I0099009

Know Yourself Phlegmatic

by Alexander Carberry

COPYRIGHT
KNOW YOURSELF PHLEGMATIC

© Alexander Carberry 2024

First Edition published by:

Bahr Press

Cross Street Business Centre

43a Cross Street

Suite 10

Burton-upon-Trent

Staffordshire

DE14 3AR

United Kingdom

All rights reserved. No part of this publication may be reproduced, stored in any retrieval system or transmitted in any form or by any means, electronic, mechanical, photocopying, recording or otherwise without the prior permission of the publishers.

Written by: Alexander Carberry

Editor: Uthman Ibrahim-Morisson

Cover photograph: © ??

Cover Design: Khadijah Carberry

A catalogue record of this book is available from the British Library.

ISBN-13: 978-0-9564513-5-4

About the Author

Alex Carberry was born in London England and was raised in Guyana South America on the edge of the Amazon. He returned to the United Kingdom to study but after meeting with a Sufi teacher chose instead to embark upon the Sufic path. He has spent 30 years studying Sufism, philosophy, geo-politics and Daoist martial arts. He is a practising herbalist and resides in Burton-upon-Trent, England

Dedication

To H. Abdurrahman Heron, my teacher, who became my companion. A laughing lion in whom wildness, generosity, nobility, courage, growth and change remain alive. He has held me to this Know Yourself series and always asked for this final book and it was in conversation with him that I first caught a clear vision of the consuming intellectual encirclement of ideology. Thank you for your encouragement and support. Below is his advice and example.

So flee to Allah!

The Noble Quran (51:50)

Contents

Dedication   **2**

Introduction   **1**

A Phlegmatic is a Phlegmatic   3

Apple Trees Do Not Produce Bananas   6

The Forest and the Trees   8

What You Will Get From This Book   9

Let Others Be What They Are   11

How To Read This Book   12

Welcome to the Journey   14

The Pure Phlegmatic   **17**

A Picture of the Phlegmatic   17

Phlegmatic Relationships   20

Phlegmatic Strategies   30

If I Watch You Long Enough, I'll See Right Through
You   30

Inaction Is Always Better Than Action   32

The Phlegmatic in Love   36

The Phlegmatic Friend   37

Invest in Relationships   42

The Phlegmatic at Work   45

Phlegmatic at Play   47

The Phlegmatic Student   49

Eight Tips for Engaging Curiosity During Study
52

Phlegmatic Learning and Study Style   55

Phlegmatic Decision Making   56

Phlegmatic Communication   59

Making Your Needs Known and Understood   63

The Phlegmatic in Company   63

4 Things Which Help Your Energetic Protection 64

Silence   65

Ways to Decompress   66

5 First Steps   67

20 Ways to Make a Break For It With Excellent
Excuses   68

21 Ways to Decompress   71

Don't Be Guilty About Being an Introvert   74

Presentations and Public Speaking   74

6 Reasons Why You Should Share Your Views
and Insights   76

16 Ways Phlegmatics Can Motivate Themselves
For Public Speaking   78

Why Dealing With Crowds is Important   82

8 Uses of Crowds   84

Phlegmatic Choosing a Profession   88

I Want to Make a Difference to the World   89

Apprehension   91

Creativity 92

Phlegmatic Friend 93

Phlegmatic in Love 98

The World According to the Phlegmatic 100

CV 102

Things I Hate 104

My Outlook 104

The Phlegmatic According to the Rest of the World 105

The Good Points 105

The Complaints 106

Spot The Phlegmatic 107

Summary 109

The Mixes **113**

Introduction 113

The Phlegmatic Forest 118

The Phlegmatic-Sanguine **121**

The World According to the Phlegmatic
Sanguine   122

The Phlegmatic-Sanguine According to the
World   127

The Phlegmatic-Sanguine Impulses   128

Summary   129

The Phlegmatic-Choleric   **131**

The World According to the Phlegmatic-
Choleric   133

The Phlegmatic-Choleric Traits in The Eyes of
the World   135

The Phlegmatic-Choleric Impulses   136

Summary   137

The Phlegmatic-Melancholic   **139**

The Phlegmatic-Melancholic Traits in The Eyes
of the World   142

The Phlegmatic-Melancholic Impulses   143

Summary   144

Putting It All Together   **145**

Introduction

Welcome! You've read Know Yourself: Discover Your True Nature with the Ancient Sufis' Wisdom, you've taken the time to reflect on it, and you've really begun to feel the way that this works. You're a Phlegmatic and as time has gone on you've become more certain of it. Sometimes there just isn't the time and space you need to keep sitting, reflecting and looking at these things as you would like, but some reflection just naturally happens with you and your intuition on your specific type and the other types and this keeps growing. By now, you probably want to continue the journey and delve more deeply into your own type.

If you're not a Phlegmatic, then prepare for a dive into the deep oceans, rivers and lakes of this Water Element type. You will learn about what flows beneath the calm inscrutable surface of this type. You will learn why they are so often and so easily overlooked, and if you are a Phlegmatic you will realise that this is a superpower, if perhaps you haven't realised this already. As a Phlegmatic you probably worked out your type fairly quickly, but you've doubts as to whether your traits and qualities are actually strengths. Don't worry, let's see what you think by the end of the book.

You've a genius for quiet observation and this book will help you to see the textures, patterns and rhythms of yourself more clearly. I don't need to teach you much about the art of people watching, but seeing ourselves clearly is a really difficult business. Apple trees produce apples and they don't produce pears, but apples are of many types, and again by the end of the book, you'll be able to distinguish between the different types of Phlegmatic.

Our hidden music wafts through us all and as you have probably figured out, Phlegmatic, in all those things around us also. You've probably figured out even the pets; your cat is a Sanguine and your dog a Melancholic. And If you don't have pets you can't resist the opportunity to

2

observe the pets of others. This is just the way that the Phlegmatic is wired. The thing is, Phlegmatic, that you seem to see the hidden music blowing, even through the air! A Phlegmatic is a Phlegmatic and this is just the way that you are wired.

A Phlegmatic is a Phlegmatic

Phlegmatics are in harmony with the Element of Water. Water reveals so much about you, it is soft, cool, flows gently, clears, cleans and clarifies things, it seeks the lowest point, at rest it is smooth mirror-like and reflective, it cools things down and nurtures life. Water nurtures life but conceals an awesome and sometimes destructive power which is shocking to behold and must be respected. We cook our food, quench our thirst, wash, cool engines, water our crops, drive hydro-powered turbines and sail our ships, upon and with water. It is revealing that in English water is also a verb, so we water our crops, are watered by knowledge and in this sense watering also means to nurture. Water nurtures and conceals its awesome destructive power as those who have witnessed this power during floods may attest. Soft, gentle water conceals great power which we harness in hydro-power. Water's power is diffuse, it spreads and it seeks the lowest point.

It generates and clarifies. It clarifies and purifies. Your energetic signature and purpose as a phlegmatic is very similar. The season you are in harmony with is winter, and you are as winter. Winter stills, stripping back the leaves, concentrating the sap of the tree deep into the trunk and the roots, and prepares in its underground for the vast flowering of spring. Winter is cold, slows life down and concentrates activity into the hidden aspects of life. The spring and summer stand upon the clarifying and nurturing inner power of winter. It teaches us that in apparent outer stillness there is nurturing and necessary activity hidden in the depths. In winter damp and wetness predominate, the cold clings and food is scarce. Many animals hibernate at this time. And the overwhelming power of freezing is apparent. People seek warmth and comfort and slow down their activity. The power of freezing forces people to become still and reflective.

Phlegmatics are like this, you'll see vast variety amongst them but they are deep, reflective waters, listening, reflecting, relaxing, waiting and observing. They are not very goal oriented but rather prefer to enjoy the journey, go with the flow and see where they end up. They listen easily and deeply and people feel heard in their presence, they will listen and observe from the sidelines, they let your arguments and observations emerge and are not fond of unnecessarily committing to action, they prefer to go with the flow. Their underlying harmonies with the Element of Water and the winter Season bestow deep wisdom to Phlegmatics. These harmonies reveal your phlegmatic purpose and natural strengths and weaknesses. We will really explore the Phlegmatic and various Phlegmatic combinations in the book. I promise that you will discover more about yourself than you would perhaps like to know and that the other types reading this book will discover much more about you than you would perhaps like to reveal. You'll discover things about yourself that you will like, and if I do my job right, a fair bit that you may hate but that is the joy of self discovery, some of it is quite uncomfortable and some of it you may be quite proud of, but in the end it is all you, and you have no choice but to embrace it all. You, Phlegmatic, are not new to the Earth and as all Phlegmatics before you, you are facing the challenges that Phlegmatics have always faced. Take heart and consolation in that, for you are not the first and many of the Phlegmatics before you have thrived.

When Rainer Maria Rilke said, "I am learning to see. I don't know why it is, but everything enters me more deeply and doesn't stop where it once used to. I have an interior that I never knew of." I am forced to think, how phlegmatic! Except that the Phlegmatic was always aware and knew the depth of their interior. Yes, Rilke was definitely not a Phlegmatic.

You are a Phlegmatic and that is just the way that you are wired!

Apple Trees Do Not Produce Bananas

Yes, apple trees do not produce bananas! We all know this! When people ask me whether they can change their type, I think, "You are suggesting that banana trees should produce apples!". *You* are utterly *you* and thank God this will not change, get over it. Learning to work with the nature that you have been allotted is your life's task. You will not change your fundamental self, that is a futile effort, but as for learning to work with the nature that you already have and bringing the best out of yourself? Now, this is very possible and it will teach you wisdom. Your fundamental nature gives you space within which to slide comfortably into your skin. A nurturing activity that waters those deep gifts hidden within your depths. There, deep within your patterning are immense gifts that even now you take for granted and may not value, but you,

Phlegmatic, possess superpowers that you habitually overlook. Your flowing, changing energetic signature expresses itself and is often so transparent that it is hard to see, but once you know how to look you will always spot the signature of the Phlegmatic. Just as when we only have to hear a few notes in order to immediately recognise the music of Beyonce, Amy Winehouse, Sarah Vaughan, Dinah Washington, Maria Callas or Paul Robeson, or the unmistakable aura of an Ousmane Sembène film after glimpsing a single languid scene; in the same way that you recognise their signature, yours Phlegmatic, is always apparent also. Your energetic pattern sings through everything that you do and that you are. It is clear from the tenor of your voice and the sound and pattern of your footsteps. It is you and you are it. Those who love it in us will love it, and those who hate it in us will hate it. Good luck to them! We are certainly not here to please everyone! Your life is your song and not theirs. This is the way that you are made, Phlegmatic, and though you may refine and shape so much of yourself, you are what you are and thank God for that. As you will see in this book there is so much more to you than initially meets the eye. So by all means, change, grow and nurture your gifts but recognise that you, Phlegmatic, are Phlegmatic and that gift is here to stay. William Shakespeare puts these powerful words into the mouth of Hamlet, "To thine own self be true, and it must follow, as the night the day, thou canst not then be false to any man." And Oh, Phlegmatic, not being true to yourself makes you very sick, very quickly.

You are what you are and your personality type is the energetic description of your psyche, which is from the Greek word for breath, its Sufic equivalent is the Arabic word *ruh* (pronounced roo -h), which also means breath. Both the Greek word *psyche* and the Arabic word *ruh* refer to the soul. So, Phlegmatic, I invite you to peer into the patterning of your very soul. Apple trees do not produce bananas and that is just the way it is.

The Forest and the Trees

A personality type is like a forest of birch trees. Though all birch trees are remarkably similar and they are from the same family of trees, every one of them is unique. Amongst them are groups of birches that possess similar traits. In this book I will show you the various types of Phlegmatics and how they differ.

What You Will Get From This Book

Since this book is about Phlegmatics, expect it to deliver just that. If you want the details of the other types then read:

- Know Yourself
- Know Yourself Sanguine
- Know Yourself Choleric
- Know Yourself Melancholic

What we will develop in this book is the ability to look at ourselves in the manner that an artist may look at a painting. With attention to the details, seeing the brushstrokes, the hues, tones and richness of colour. We get the feel of the proportions, the composition and the perspective. Then, when you know your art, you will be able to say this is Chéri Samba, Ibrahim El-Salahi or a 'Afi' Ekong. You will develop the art of feeling through the texture of your own personality, and these skills will serve you well as you observe others. These will be your skills forever and you will be able to rely on them to open up your greatest and truest wealth, for within yourself, your intuition is a gift to the world. Knowing yourself, teaches and enables you to know others.

You will gain insights into the intricacies of your own personality and some of this will be difficult to swallow but we will explore how to turn this to your advantage. You will discover and plumb your own natural genius – that is, *'genius'* used in the original Latin sense of 'your natural inclination or natural abilities'. You have a genius and there is not another genius like yours in the universe. Learning to work with your genius and standing in your strengths and avoiding or making use of your weaknesses, will teach you to engage your natural strategic advantages. There are areas in which you are naturally weak, and when you enter them you must be clear about that and have a plan, in order to avoid the pain of the inevitable issues that arise from these natural areas of weakness. For those who are not Phlegmatics, you want tips on how to deal with difficult Phlegmatics. I will do my best to share what I can with you, but remember that like water, Phlegmatics tend to slip away. This will take skill. I want you to be the best that you can be, and so I will share whatsoever I can to help you achieve this. This series is short and easy to read, you should be able to read one of these books quickly and smoothly. So, within these limits, I will share as much as I can.

Let Others Be What They Are

People are just the way they are and you don't have to be convinced, you just have to keep trying to change their basic natures for the futility of this exercise to become crystal clear to you. People are wired the way that they are and I am sure that by the end of this book, you won't be able to keep holding onto the idea that people can be moulded like clay into whatever you wish them to be. Evolution, progress, toxicity and whatever else you choose to call it, people are people and working with the way that they actually are will always give better results than working with people according to the way you think they should be. If this triggers you I understand, but bear this in mind and see how the journey goes for you. Learning to accept ourselves and others is a major hurdle on the way to wisdom. Because accepting this allows us to get on with the job of dealing with ourselves. We give ourselves permission to be ourselves and this enables us to allow others to be themselves. Yes, we can strengthen natural strengths, learn to deal with natural weaknesses, and we can politely tell others off for their bad habits, but just remember that we are what we are, and if you are determined to make a swan out of a wolf you will be eternally disappointed. The odds are just stacked against you. Let's not tyrannise ourselves and others and learn to work with ourselves and each other as we all really are.

How To Read This Book

Go through the contents page and take a quick look at what arouses your interest. Your attention to that which interests you will begin to build connections and motivate you to read the book. Yes, you'll get an idea of the book's structure but this is not as interesting to Phlegmatics as other types. You'll get a feel for the book and this will encourage you to read it. Then you may read through the book once quickly or just focus upon the bits that interest you. Reading through once completely will help to give you context, then you'll know where to find the relevant parts when you need them.

Observe the ideas, concepts and patterns in those around you. Really enjoy this because as a Phlegmatic people watching is important to you. Find ways of sharing the observations and patterns that you become aware of with those around you who are willing to listen. Question those around you, who have known you for a long time to find out how they really see you. Observe the patterns and especially the differences in how you and others do what you do and how you think about things. Truth can often be bitter at first but it is the fabric of reality and it is easier to deal with the truth than to engage with illusions. Bitterness becomes sweeter with time. You don't have to like it, but you would do better to surrender to the way things actually are, rather than futilely fighting losing battles. Also, delusion is already a loss. This is some of the most transformative work that we will ever do. However much we may dislike it, blueness is blueness and it will not be transformed. We may change the shade, tone and hue of the colour blue, but blueness will always remain its permanent feature. Our fundamental nature is analogous to colouring in this respect. Read the book, make your observations and once they become clear to you, accept them. Acceptance is not such a difficult step, but neither is it easy. We can tell ourselves stories about ourselves and our world, but they are just stories; the way things are, transcends and shatters our stories. Over time we learn that our dislike and resistance to the way things are, will change to acceptance. At that point you are free. You are free to work with what is there, rather than attempting to delude yourself by entertaining illusions. Over time and with gentle practice our need to persist with our favourite stories in the face of reality diminishes.

Welcome to the Journey

Congratulations, you have made it this far. Let us continue our journey into the phlegmatic depths. Let us uncover the treasures, wonderful surprises and fascinating wonders there lying in wait to be discovered. This knowledge continues to fascinate me and I am always excited to share it with you. I hope that you will be even more fascinated than I have been, and I pray that you will continue to find it more and more useful as you continue to work with your true self.

The amazing thing about the Universe is that the realisations, observations and reflections that have changed you have also transformed the Universe. Yes, read that again. You change the Universe by changing yourself. Everything is in change and yet everything remains the same. Transformation is in the very fabric of the Universe, and you are an integral part of it. You are the little universe and the Universe is the big you, and beyond that there is realisation. You were born to be what you are, so be the best that you can be.

> So which of your Lord's blessings
> do you both deny?

Everyone in the heavens and earth requests His aid.

Every day He is engaged in some affair.

So which of your Lord's blessings do you both deny?

The Noble Qur'an: 55:28-30

The Pure Phlegmatic

A Picture of the Phlegmatic

You are like water and winter. What characterises winter characterises you: coolness, stillness, quietness, reflectiveness, hibernation, conserving the stored fruits, muted colours, considering your options, conservation of energy in the cold of winter days, activity hidden below the surface and reflection. Winter is the pinnacle of stillness and coolness, and once the pinnacle of contraction is reached the creation moves naturally into activity and expansion, the stillness is necessary to sustain the activity of the hot months. Phlegmatics are aware of this reality intuitively and their actions are always in harmony with this. Their movements are smooth, flowing, almost circular, and they flow into things, with the easy gliding movements of a fish. Phlegmatics do not stand out, they prefer to fade into the background, in muted beautifully coordinated colours, like blues, turquoises, and pastel greens. Once on the move they avoid unnecessary eye contact and observe from the sidelines, but always with flowing motions. You, Phlegmatic, usually shift your weight to the back foot, in a naturally defensive stance, and you use this posture to maintain distance between you and others. You will slip away if people invade your space when you don't invite them in. You also sit in this manner. This is the music singing through you like a gentle breeze, in a manner that only Phlegmatics can. Understanding how this music is heard by other types will be a valuable lesson for you. The hotter types will become frustrated by their inability to pin you down, and they will find you too quiet, and able to slip too easily through their fingers like water. Your natural evasiveness infuriates them and this is your superpower.

Your attitude is relaxed and easy going, and just like water and winter you are nurturing, but it is hidden beneath the surface, in the deep, concealed underneath and often hidden from even the one being nurtured. You must learn to harmonise with this hidden music and let the Phlegmatic rhythm move you harmoniously in just such a smooth, hidden, unassuming way so that the flowers and growth of spring happen when the seasons are right. The Choleric marshals and you nurture and allow things to grow naturally into maturity and you do this with as little confrontation as possible. The Phlegmatic genius is a glorious thing to behold, and learning to let this flow through you will let your genius flow into the world. You will learn mastery of this power by a lifetime of harmony, reflection, study, and just letting things happen. Being Phlegmatic is a great mystery that may lead to great wisdom, if you dare to let it be. You tend to seek inner mastery and may mistakenly assume that inner mastery of the flow of this connected water energy is sufficient, but you are tested with outward action in the world to give form to the currents which flow in your depths. This discipline is the zone of mastery for without mastery of yourself, you will be frustrated and your energy will turn inward towards the abyss and I think that you will agree that being unable to climb out of the abyss leaves you feeling trapped and hopeless.

> Life is a balance between holding
> on and letting go!
> **Rumi**

Since you are like water it is instructive to reflect upon what happens when water lies still and stagnant, the passive power of water requires movement, whereas fire's nature is active and moving, and if it is to be used safely it must be rooted and stilled, water's still power is bound to its need for movement. Observe

19

rivers and bodies of water and study them. See how naturally their tiny ecosystems arise as water flows through the terrain and see what happens when water is still, see how and what invades and know that your genius comes at a price. To healthily find balance with your genius you must seek movement even though you may not want to do this. This is a fundamental Phlegmatic test. When water moves it clarifies and purifies and when it is stagnant it gives life to that which does not. Looking at water, being around water, being absorbed in water, staring at water and drinking water are all important to your holistic health.

Remember that whilst water conceals potential it requires movement to bring that hidden potential into being, if you do not pay heed to this your deeply hidden energetic reserves may turn upon you.

Phlegmatic Relationships

In relationships you listen, you nurture and avoid conflict. You feel compelled to listen and have a tendency to see the other point of view or rather, points of view. This makes it hard to take decisive, definitive decisions. You don't let people into your private zone unless you want to or need to and you find prolonged closeness difficult, as this will often leave you feeling trapped and claustrophobic. You don't like to be contained as this will make you feel constricted and will often elicit a strong visceral response. Your capacity for feelings becomes easily overwhelmed and this will often leave you quite confused about your own feelings; meaning that you can find it hard to distinguish between your emotions and the emotions and feelings you sense from others. This is the unexpected price of your incredible intuition and empathy.

Your display of emotions tends to be muted, and you don't react well to being smothered and will view the expression of excessive emotional displays and interaction as overwhelming and perhaps even smothering of your own sense of self. You can tend to be suspicious of the emotional intrusion, though at times you like to cuddle and be close, but it is better when you initiate this. Water joins together, especially when used as a solvent and you will quietly bring people together but like water you seek the lowest point and this is your immense strength. The Arabs have a saying, 'The servant is the master of people.' This becomes very apparent with Phlegmatics. People depend upon you and often don't even realise what you do, because like water you are almost transparent, you evade being seen quite effortlessly, but they will often depend upon your opinion and insight. This transparency allows others to see each other in your presence without you getting in the way, you facilitate this, in a non-threatening and comfortable way. However, you view this as service and not as mastery (that would be the Choleric!). The importance of water tends to be overlooked and that is precisely why water is so powerful and indispensable. You will often be taken for granted.

Water sinks and calms, it supports and allows things to float. Your affection tends to be quite cool headed, and you tend to utilise the activeness of the other party to encourage them to come into your zone and as a result, more often than not, you end up in relationships with hot types.

As a Phlegmatic you are very intuitive, you know closely, from within the threads of the fibres, with a capacity for an intimate grasp of the states of others. Often you expect others to know as you know, without needing to say it. It is perhaps for this reason that you don't discuss certain things, in fact you don't see the point of discussing it because doesn't everyone get this? But they don't. Getting you to speak up and speak out about your deep feelings, needs and moods is difficult and often you will just listen because listening is easier. The Choleric will speak up and make things known and you often find this abrasive, the Melancholic will talk around things in a most cerebral and sometimes convoluted way that no one but a reader of runes can work out, and then the Sanguine will just spill their guts in order to make clear what they have to say, because they scarcely know anything unless they speak it. You, on the other hand, just know it but find it difficult to speak it. Avoiding the limelight and communicative evasiveness are two of your natural strategies. You effortlessly slip through their fingers or just don't engage, but it isn't that you refuse to engage, you just remain unengaged. These are natural tactics which you just know. No one ever had to teach you these strategies.

You'll often agree with someone to get them off your back and then remain diffuse and unengaged. You don't need to twist and turn, for when they come to engage and pin you down there is just nothing there. This water strategy is unbelievably effective. Water is by its nature powerful and underestimated. People find it difficult to take a stand against you because there's nothing to take a stand against. You remain out of reach even when you are within range. Furthermore, your capacity to listen, causes people to readily shift their attention back to themselves, for water is also a mirror. This aspect of yourself gives others clarity. Your nature is also calming and non-threatening and so your aqueousness inspires the water in others.

You are reflective and you avoid unnecessary commitment. Like winter you conserve your energy. This allows you to reflect and ask yourself questions about life, activity and the meaning of existence. Your quiet reflectivity is perceived by others as inscrutability; they just can't work you out. Those who invest in learning how to speak to you and how to be with you, will derive immense benefit. They gain an insight in which they may see their own reflection, some may hate what they see and in these cases it is easier to hate you than it is to confront themselves. Water is the Element which is at the foundations of the Universe, it is the Element closest to the Aether, the undifferentiated abyss at the foundations of the Worlds, in the descent of reality into the manifest realms, Elemental Water emerges as the first Element in the emergence of Aether into the manifest physicality of the world. You, Phlegmatic, remain attached to the abyss at the foundational centre of the world, and hence, for many you are undifferentiated and unknowable. Please remember this in relationships for you will have to speak them into your reality so that they may have a chance of empathising with you.

Relationships are a collaboration, but remember that with Phlegmatics they are Elemental Water and all life comes to the watering hole to drink. Paying attention to the dynamics of the relationship and the need for gratitude increases the depth of relationships, and this increases what is present to be grateful for. If you don't, irreconcilable differences in opinion and state will appear and the relationship becomes unsustainable. Remember that in Phlegmatic relationships the harmony of state is very important, because much of Phlegmatic communication is non-verbal and intuitive. And remember that the passive rarely initiates. The challenge for the Phlegmatic is connecting across the gulf in relating with other types, especially since you are quite self contained. And for others it is the challenge of learning to tease the self contained Phlegmatic self out into the open plains beyond the abyss. These relationships are a lifetime of work and for the Phlegmatic in particular, they require courage. It is often easier to disappear into the abyss.

If you are in a relationship with a Phlegmatic you will have to reach into the abyss to find their concealed self and you will not glimpse its jewels unless you learn to dive deep, whilst not being invasive. You will be surprised at their imaginativeness and quiet, fun-loving nature. But if you want to reach into the depths you must learn to explore without drawing attention to yourself. The fruits are hidden beneath ice and snow, often deep in caves beneath their upper layers. They are naturally suspicious and shy of those who begin to explore their deep domains, so they have to welcome you in, and you have to be inconspicuous, so that they may almost notice you as if not noticing that you are there, whilst being able to leave you alone, to observe you quietly from the safe distance of their sidelines. The more you draw attention to yourself within their zone, the more likely they are to withdraw into their own space. Remember that they have to allow you to enter their habitat and this is a deeply intimate concession, so Phlegmatics must feel comfortable and safe with you.

Later in the day is the best time for Phlegmatics. They warm up slowly throughout the day and need room to start gradually, they may not reach their optimum until the warmer hours of the day. Give them space in the mornings to warm up and become clear. They have a natural rhythm, so learn to work with it. Phlegmatic-Choleric often differ in this. As a Phlegmatic you must move and heat your core in the morning, allowing yourself to gradually seize the day. Think of a stream gradually gathering momentum downhill until it becomes a waterfall. Use the gradient of the day and activity to gather momentum and to surf the current of the day. Don't interrupt Phlegmatics once they are in flow as flow is hard for them to attain, and over time this will irritate them. Observe them and figure out the signals that indicate they want to engage and especially the signs that they don't want to engage.

For a Phlegmatic to respect you fully you have to learn to listen. As a Phlegmatic it is useful to learn to teach people who have committed to you, how to work with you. Your signals are quite muted to the hot types so you may have to amplify them somewhat.

If you are tired, stressed, emotionally imbalanced and feel stuck, you will tend to fall back into the abyss. It is as if you lose the energy and the will to climb out. You lose the will and the energy for social relations and you cease to participate. From here you can fall deeper and deeper into the void and for those around you, you become less and less

27

accessible, disappearing into the darkest depths, where you may become overwhelmed by pessimism and loss of hope. This is your reflexive response: you seek refuge in the abyss as if crawling back into the womb. If you have fallen in due to exhaustion then you must rest before you can find the energy to crawl back out. However if exhaustion is not the cause, then you may seek refuge but you must practise the steps up and out of these deep valleys on a daily basis whether you like it or not. You don't have to spend a long time outside of the safety of the abyss. This movement will help you to see your way through the world and it is necessary, for within the abyss everything falls back into you. Whilst coming out and going in gives life to a very different mode of vision. Yes you must rest but, Phlegmatic you must also climb.

When you are in love, you give very faint signals and the few that you do give, you expect them to be seen, whilst hoping that they are not, but whilst also expecting that they are. It drives you mad, much less an outsider! You'll accept them in, scarcely invite them in, expect them to know, be pessimistic about it, not expecting it to work, but know that it should. The poor suitor will have their work cut out for themselves but once they get in it is welcoming, imaginative, calming, nurturing and quiet. Occasionally, you will make your affections known, gently but passionately, but at other times you will be evasive. Vulnerability is dealt with by staying out of reach but when it deepens the relationship and you feel safe there will be moments when you skydive into disclosure and will wonder whether you have said too much. But perhaps this is because you say so little.

If you're pursuing a Phlegmatic, good luck! You will have your work cut out for you. You will really have to increase the subtlety of your interpersonal skills. I'm praying for you but I'll also share some highly valuable tips in this book.

Phlegmatic - remember, that you need to welcome them across the bridge if you want the relationship, and yes, them crossing the bridge buys you ample time to observe them and to make up your mind. Or better still, if they make it across the bridge and through the woods then they might be worth the effort.

Phlegmatic Strategies

If I Watch You Long Enough, I'll See Right Through You

Phlegmatics watch from the sidelines, from the cover of the bushes, always in perfect natural camouflage. They see below the surface, they watch for the hidden swells and impulses and grasp the natural spontaneity of the target in question. And they don't need to learn how to do this, it's hardwired into them. They watch most often without ulterior motives. The Art of People Watching and inscrutability are Phlegmatic pastimes. Conserving energy and a healthy scepticism about the effectiveness of doing something is the Phlegmatic default. Accept that this is a part of the Phlegmatic personality and that there is nothing inherently wrong with this impulse. In fact it is an important part of Phlegmatic growth and the path to Phlegmatic wisdom.

As a Phlegmatic you just look, you don't have to try, and so please use your acute genius for observation well. If you desire to avoid being landed in situations that just force decisions upon you and land you into spaces of entrapment, then you must recognise that you have to act appropriately. You have a choice and not choosing is a choice, even a choice about choices; you cannot escape the consequences. Remember that your penchant for patient observation and dislike of unnecessary action will not be shared by many of those around you and you will be criticised for this. There are other types and the difference amongst types and their natural contrasts are part of what we must expect. In your case you will tend to feel your way into a decision, and where the Choleric will just know, you just feel that it is right. Learning to trust this and work with it is important. Cholerics have judgement whilst your strength is intuition. Judgement makes decisions easy and intuition often does the opposite, for the companion of intuition is empathy and from a position of empathy it becomes difficult to decide. For you, learning to develop a relationship with judgement is also important for it enables you to act, when necessary. On your journey you have to have times when you act and when you observe. You don't have a problem with forcing yourself to stop and refuel; you have to look long enough to see what a natural and sustainable rhythm must be and then find ways of flexibly sticking with it. Your natural curiosity is a very useful motivation which if you engage with, it will keep you motivated. And yes, you need to enjoy the journey rather than just relentlessly driving towards a goal.

Inaction Is Always Better Than Action

Therefore the sage manages affairs without doing anything,

and conveys his instructions without the use of speech.

All things spring up, and there is not one which declines to show itself;

they grow, and there is no claim made for their ownership;

they go through their processes, and there is no expectation (of a reward for the results).

The work is accomplished, and there is no resting in it (as an achievement).

The work is done, but how no one can see;

'Tis this that makes the power not cease to be.

-- Tao te Ching, Lao Tze

The Phlegmatic seems to know this way of knowing implicitly. This isn't a strategy but a deep way of being hardwired into them. They are comfortable with inaction and grasp the deep power of letting things take their course. The more you interfere, the more you must do, and the less you interfere, the less you will need to do, whilst things will follow their own course anyway. Rivers flow as they do and people do what they must. Phlegmatics possess a capacity for deep reflection, observation and an empathy with the deep tidal nature of existence. Often they are not very attached to outcomes but will accept what comes, and they often don't mind not being mentioned. By way of comparison, the Choleric's obsession with fixing the outcomes of events often looks like stupidity to Phlegmatics, whilst the Melancholic's obsession with calculating the outcomes of events often looks like a punishment. On the other hand, the Sanguine's determined dreaming of desirable outcomes seems outright insane. Being possessed by the outcome, gives rise to an anxiety which compels you to seek possession; it is not the thing that possesses you, but your possession by the desired outcome that takes possession of you. The Phlegmatic sees beyond this in silence and inaction. By not preferring outward movement they see into the inward movements and seem to generally prefer what actually happens rather than that which is expected. This is why,

> All things spring up, and there is not one which declines to show itself;
>
> they grow, and there is no claim made for their ownership;
>
> they go through their processes, and there is no expectation (of a reward for the results).
>
> The work is accomplished, and there is no resting in it (as an achievement).
>
> **-- Tao te Ching, Lao Tze**

Often a knowledge path for Phlegmatics cannot be separated from a wisdom path. It has to feel whole. This is perhaps why Phlegmatics often offer such clarity as their Elemental Water nature indicates. They are more prone to releasing than holding on. So when Lao Tze says, 'He diminishes it and again diminishes it, till he arrives at doing nothing (on purpose).'...He has nailed the Phlegmatic.

(Forgetting knowledge)

He who devotes himself to learning (seeks) from day to day to increase (his knowledge);

he who devotes himself to the Dao (seeks) from day to day to diminish (his doing).

He diminishes it and again diminishes it, till he arrives at doing nothing (on purpose).

Having arrived at this point of non-action, there is nothing which he does not do.

> He who gets as his own all under heaven does so by giving himself no trouble (with that end).
>
> If one takes trouble (with that end), he is not equal to getting as his own all under heaven.
> **-- Tao te Ching, Lao Tze**

The challenge for the Phlegmatic is knowing exactly when to act and mastering how to act decisively. When the Phlegmatic masters this, it is by the maxim, 'Inaction is always better than action'.

The Phlegmatic in Love

Quite often, you won't even notice them, unless you spot them observing you from the sidelines, or beyond. You are expected to go in pursuit and generally with very little encouragement. They will listen to you, but they listen to everyone and they may be a bit awkward but they are like that anyway. If you're in pursuit then you've got your work cut out, and don't expect alot of encouragement. They nurture and listen with ease, and are naturally shy. If they start speaking to you, shut up and listen and if you want a relationship that can last, then you will have to learn to listen deeply, because you won't often get those opportunities. If they decide to evade you and not engage then you will find it impossible to pin them down. For this is their superpower. If you find yourself on this end of the matter, go for the long game, be patient, take your time and trust the process. Just remember that they see you, even if they won't let you know. They respect the process, so trust the process.

Oh yes, and Phlegmatics are affectionate. Now if that confuses you then know that they often show their affection by nurturing. Learn to recognise their boundaries because once they start to protect themselves from you they are inordinately difficult to access.

The Phlegmatic Friend

Expect to be listened to, to experience empathy, diplomacy and often not to be certain where you stand. The focus will invariably be upon you and you will often be expected to take the initiative. They will understand almost every position you have and hear you. And if they tell you off, it will rarely be in a fit of anger for your first or second or third infraction. Usually you will have done repeatedly exactly what it is you're being told off for. They want you to speak your mind and they will hear where you're coming from and their comments will often be neutral, wise and incisive. They avoid arguments and clashes, have acute hearing and so will tend to dislike you being loud. The energetic attraction around Phlegmatics is usually that you're attracted into their orbit and you approach and make your way into their sphere.

Phlegmatics love you speaking your mind but dislike disagreements and turmoil. Phlegmatics can accept different positions and they may often seem to be radically opposing positions to you, but not to them. This is because they view your intellectual positions like windows looking onto a matter, they rarely mistake the idea for the thing and so they accept that it is possible to hold many differing positions about the same thing. This is in part the secret of their capacity for tolerance.

(The nourishment of the person)

All in the world know the beauty of the beautiful,

and in doing this they have (the idea of) what ugliness is;

they all know the skill of the skilful,

and in doing this they have (the idea of) what the want of skill is.

So it is that existence and non-existence give birth the one to (the idea of) the other;

that difficulty and ease produce the one (the idea of) the other;

that length and shortness fashion out the one the figure of the other;

that (the ideas of) height and lowness arise from the contrast of the one with the other;

that the musical notes and tones become harmonious through the relation of one with another;

and that being before and behind give the idea of one following another.

-- Tao te Ching, Lao Tze

Phlegmatics really grasp this and are flexible at looking from differing perspectives. Where Cholerics will think that you cannot be that smart if you disagree with them, Phlegmatics want to understand where you are coming from. They are inherently curious about the way that you work. They tend to apologise easily and will think of you, your perspective and your feelings. The cost of this is that they tend to dwell in spaces of observation and letting things happen.

> Therefore the sage manages affairs without doing anything,
>
> and conveys his instructions without the use of speech.
>
> All things spring up, and there is not one which declines to show itself;
>
> they grow, and there is no claim made for their ownership;

they go through their processes, and there is no expectation (of a reward for the results).

The work is accomplished, and there is no resting in it (as an achievement).

The work is done, but how no one can see;

'Tis this that makes the power not cease to be.

-- Tao te Ching, Lao Tze

If your focus is doing, then you will tend to see them as lazy, if your focus is understanding, then you will glimpse their easygoing, insightful genius.

If you wish to build a relationship with a Phlegmatic then you will have to learn to work with them as they are, not as you think they should be.

As a Phlegmatic it is useful to have some prickly friends who understand you and protect your boundaries, you nurture and they protect but then you must understand the dynamics of the

relationship and you can't consciously
recognise this unless you learn to recognise and
protect your own boundaries. Deeply nurturing
relationships aren't transactional but they have
their dynamics, and learning to work with them
in ways that they protect your weaknesses is
part of what you naturally do anyway. I'm just
suggesting that you be conscious about it.

Invest in Relationships

Phlegmatics have an eye on the present and the
past, since for them the past relates to the
future. The future for them is as it relates to the
past and so they reflect on your past actions
and what animates them and will expect your
future actions to be based upon your behaviour
in the past. They dwell only fleetingly in the
future, for the past and the now are more
important to them. They enjoy reminiscing and
talking about what's happening, and may find
conversations which always dwell upon what
you will do, especially if there is no
precedence, irritating. They are usually not that
bothered with you bringing up past mistakes
and will often laugh at themselves but if you do
that then be prepared for some apposite
reminders of what you also did, and if you are
too thin skinned to handle that, then you'd
better leave their faults alone. Yes they noticed

them and their silence was out of consideration for you.

As a Phlegmatic you need access to relationships that grant you vision into other ways of seeing, you instinctively know this but this is about consciously engaging with this to strengthen your natural genius for observation and learning.

If you wish to have a strong relationship with other types, then you will have to remember that they are often not as observant as yourself, and your cool relationship vibes may just not register on their geiger counter. Occasionally you will have to give them stronger vibes to work with, so that they remain committed to doing the work.

You will naturally tend to make thousands of excuses for those around you and will often think of yourself last. Making excuses for people and empathising with them isn't that much of a test for you. What is, is! You must ensure that the people in your inner circle make excuses, consider and protect you. Water without a protective container will evaporate, water with boundaries around it becomes a river, there are lessons in that for people who reflect.

> In the creation of the heavens and the earth,
>
> And the alternation of night and day,
>
> There are Signs for people with intelligence
> -- **Al Qur'an 3:190**

Yes you are attracted to those of opposite qualities, water is cool and seeks heat, you observe and so are attracted to those who act. This is itself the essence of the Cosmic Dance.

> Every particle of the world is in love with a dance,
>
> Moving in rhythm, aligning with the cosmic trance.
>
> Earth, water, fire, and air all spin and entwine,
>
> In this dance of existence, their true forms shine.
> -- **Shams Tabriz**

The challenge in relationships is to find the hidden balance.

The Phlegmatic at Work

It has got to excite your curiosity, for though you are a cool type there is a deep hidden passion within you and it is driven by a quiet, intuitive curiosity. Boredom will cause you to collapse in upon yourself psychologically, feeling trapped and apathetic and there is not much worse for a Phlegmatic than that. If you find yourself constantly coming up with risque jokes, comments and resorting to sabotage then you're quite likely bored. The subtle, smooth, gentle, exploring energy of the Phlegmatic is fundamental to the type and it needs an arena and objects to explore. It is a creative intelligence and so bound to the creative expression of life force, if it does not have a space and objects to explore weird things happen. Do not underestimate your intelligence, its sensuousness and your need to explore, it is fundamental to you, and so incredibly easy for you to overlook. Underestimate the importance of this and this will cause you emotional and psychological harm. It is better for you if your work can provide this, and if it can't, something in your life must. What I am saying is that the challenge for you isn't motivation, it is the curse of the lack of curiosity; curiosity and quiet exploration are what motivate you. Boredom is your soul killer. And your libido often speaks it most clearly.

Working with people which has distance implicit in it, it works for you and you have the capacity to be forever fascinated by people, creative explorations and problem solving which requires subtlety really excite you. Psychology fascinates you. If you have ever read Balzac then know that he is a Phlegmatic and his writing style is utterly phlegmatic. You must feel able to explore texture, motivations, possibilities, tragedies and the complexity of the underlying structure and impulse nature of things. These things will forever interest you, and so don't mistake lack of motivation for laziness. You require subtle curiosity and exploration. And if you can get things done without being noticed this seems like heaven for you. It is not that you don't need appreciation, it is that appreciation, praise and accolades matter less than your need to creatively explore.

Learning to find and feel the moment when action is most pregnant in its result, will excite you and motivate you more than battling with procrastination. If you find yourself procrastinating, eliminate exhaustion, then examine your explorational curiosity, then fascinate yourself with timing.

Phlegmatic at Play

Phlegmatics like to play but where Cholerics play to win, Phlegmatics don't play to win first and foremost. It is not that they don't like winning but that the creative exploration is what motivates them, not just the goal itself. You need to explore the process, win with timing and in ways which seem effortless, and in which your opponent can't quite work out how it happened, and you can then poker-facedly smile inside. The motivating challenges are effortlessness, where superior timing and subtle use of technique are at a premium.

Therefore the sage manages affairs without doing anything,

and conveys his instructions without the use of speech.

All things spring up, and there is not one which declines to show itself;

they grow, and there is no claim made for their ownership;

they go through their processes, and there is no expectation (of a reward for the results).

The work is accomplished, and there is no resting in it (as an achievement).

The work is done, but how no one can see;

'Tis this that makes the power not cease to be.

-- Tao te Ching, Lao Tze

This tendency to flexibility, intuition, immersion and a hidden type of mastery provide the motivation that a Phlegmatic can admire. How you win is more important to you than winning. You must feel relaxed, it must be fun and you must be able to explore the textural difference of technique and to feel the way the opponent changes under pressure or in response to ease. You need to play with the opponent, this is completely natural to you.

The play has to be play and if you are coaching Phlegmatics you would do well to remember this. And when a Choleric or Melancholic can't quite work out how they are being beaten that is a rarified pleasure for a Phlegmatic. And there is a point in it that you may even wonder if you are a bit of a sadist, but I suspect that you won't even care. Oh, and you'll keep it a secret, and keep them guessing until they die. Sadistic?

The Phlegmatic Student

The greatest dangers for the Phlegmatic is boredom, then from boredom emotional and psychological imbalance which often lead to the loss of life balance. Exhaustion and Phlegmatics don't go well together. Phlegmatics tend to get tired early and usually need to sleep early. Rest, alone time and leisure time to reflect are necessary for Phlegmatics. If you've spent time in a closely packed classroom for hours then you will need to decompress and recharge, at least enough for your head to clear and the feeling of deep depletion can shift. The Elemental Water picks up on everything and you need time and activity to help it to clear. Without a rhythm that makes space for these things you will burn out, and burn out for Phlegmatics often feels like an internal collapse. It is as if the Elemental Water collapses into the abyss, and emptiness, a sense of being trapped and despair come rising up like a tide.

You require this fundamental base of structure like all other types. However, it is as if Phlegmatics are closer to the abyss and fall back in more easily than other types. Exhaustion doesn't do well with you at all and it almost always has immediate emotional consequences. Don't get this twisted and don't misinterpret this, put structure to your life balance back in place as quickly as possible and then see what remains, you will often be surprised that this is often enough to resolve things.

When you are in this place stimulants will tend to give you energy but make you more imbalanced. Exercise, sleep and life balance are better, more sustainable options. An occasional coffee, tea or whatever will give you a boost but it is not a long term solution.

Because Elemental Water is your element you must learn its lesson, water which remains stagnant, becomes putrid, stale and foul, you have to move but you will often feel resistance to this. This is your lifelong companion and so regular exercise and movement have to be integrated into your life. It will often resolve the experience of being crowded by people and their stuff and offer you a reset. Warm baths, saunas and deep massages are important for you. Regular pacing really suits you as stamina is your natural strength. Apply your will to establish a rhythm and regular pace, so that your creative curiosity can roam within it. You are a deadly talent at this and you solve problems in surprising ways, please trust your genius and learn to work with it. And if it is effortless then you've probably nailed it.

For the Phlegmatic student, memory is your greatest asset and you must grasp how yours works. Memory has Earth which gives it structure and the structure of memory is that it is made for us to walk vast distances and to remember landmarks which may change somewhat over the year. Its water gives fertility to its Earth, this is deep creativity, songs, poems, mythological beasts, events, its Wind is the way song, and story connects the memory journey, and its Fire is the focus needed to burn and etch the memory journey into your psyche. Different types of memory require very different emphasis on these elements and you must understand how yours works. Get a text on memory, palaces and grasp the fundamentals of memory. And why is this important? Because as a Phlegmatic you need to play and explore your knowledge creatively in order to activate your genius and to do so you need to have the elements of what you know easily available and retrievable. On your walk to decompress from the energetic strain of being surrounded by all those people, you can tap in and explore your knowledge creatively. Often your genius lies in the realm of play. Yes, I am recommending that you all learn to build and play with memory palaces you Phlegmatic students.

The Phlegmatic genius is profoundly intuitive and creative, this works best when the information and basic structure is in the memory and you may now dream, envisage and imagine. Yes, for Phlegmatics especially, your dreams are a space in which thoughts are consolidated, organised, developed and reimagined. Reimagination is incredibly important to the Phlegmatic intellect. The creativity that this entails is your canvas. Grappling with thorny ideas may be boring, long and apparently pointless, but what will motivate you through the process is the curiosity to learn to engage your curiosity.

Eight Tips for Engaging Curiosity During Study

The Eight Tips:

1. Imagine how what you are learning changes the world, then turn it upside down and imagine how this might not happen. Now you have a curiosity canvas between what can happen and what may not. Put human beings in this space interacting and living their stories, how can your learning change, nurture and improve their lives?

2. Have a working rhythm and keep returning to these imaginary spaces and integrate what you've learned into changing their lives and see what questions you have and write them down, including whatever else you will need to know in order to answer them. If there is a curriculum then try and keep on track, but you may have to add the occasional extra topic which answers questions you may have, or even intuitions that feel as if they need to be present in order for you to really feel your way around the knowledge space.

3. Find ways to play with what you know and work out how it can affect your life and make life easier for you. Formulate stories which embed this change and knowledge into your life. Quite often the more outlandish they are, the more

interesting it becomes and the greater the engagement of your curiosity and reimagination.

4. Remember a study/knowledge story before bed and see if you can dream about it. Lucid dreaming is part of your knowledge process and it will bring up from your subconscious matters that you are inherently curious about.

5. Draw pictures showing the nature of the interactions and the structure of what you know, and use colours and shapes, etc. to reflect how you feel about different aspects of what you know, and when you have questions and areas that you would like to learn more about, stick huge question marks on the page, and highlight the connections that indicate how this area that you don't know would affect what you do know and what you would like to know.

6. Try keeping voice notes discussing what you understand and the questions that you have, so that you can revise on the move by listening to yourself talk about it.

7. Don't be afraid of getting it wrong, or looking stupid. The genius of Phlegmatics is often very left field and very often

people just won't get it at first. It helps to reconcile yourself with this from early on.

8. Turn up to be curious every day because your emotional and psychological health depend upon this, Phlegmatic.

Phlegmatic Learning and Study Style

This is starting to sound repetitive. Cholerics and Sanguines learn by doing and you learn by imagining. You tend to do things after you've imagined them. Talk to others to get a sense of the way their process works so that you can compare it with your own, and also become more aware of the way that you work. You tend to start slowly and rely upon flow. Flow is your genius so understand how to find your flow and organise yourself around this, and ruthlessly block and stop anyone and anything that prevents or disrupts your flow. You discover your knowledge after learning it, and you will usually continue to rediscover it throughout your life. You don't tend to like presenting but you would do well to present your knowledge as mini-booklets. One page of annotated text, picture and story summaries. Use video voice overs and other tools for making sense of your knowledge in an integrated way. Put notes around, using colours that you love. Send messages ahead of yourself as a reminder.

Deadlines are your enemy but any enemy can be beaten. The deadline pressure mounts like water behind the wall of a dam. Get to know this phenomenon and understand how this works with you and accept it as an uncomfortable but necessary part of life. Use rhythm and flow to deal with deadlines and don't push yourself up hard against the deadline before you get to work, as some other types do, this rarely works for you. Flow is your genius, So try to work with yourself rather than against it.

Phlegmatic Decision Making

Aren't the best decisions those that make themselves? Phlegmatics tend to avoid hard decisions and very often this comes from a very different impulse place than procrastination. It may look like procrastination but it comes from a very different place.

> Therefore the sage manages affairs without doing anything,
>
> and conveys his instructions without the use of speech.

All things spring up, and there is not one which declines to show itself;

they grow, and there is no claim made for their ownership;

they go through their processes, and there is no expectation (of a reward for the results).

The work is accomplished, and there is no resting in it (as an achievement).

The work is done, but how no one can see;

'Tis this that makes the power not cease to be.

-- Tao te Ching, Lao Tze

Phlegmatics are prone to do by letting go and this is a valid way of dealing with issues and even problems. The thing is, that if you must master this way of being, then you have to know when to act and when not to act. At the time that action becomes necessary you must act effortlessly, and to act effortlessly you have to fall in love with the journey of mastery.

The Greeks had two words for time: Kairos (καιρός) and Kronos (χρόνος). Kairos is time like the weather, it is a view of time as a season. For most crops, you must plant in the spring and harvest by the autumn at the latest, or you will lose the crop. This is time as timing. Seasons repeat, so being open to the timing of time is important to knowing when to act. It allows you to connect to the musical rhythms of existence. For that you either have to participate in the timing, or to submit to the timing. Kronos is sequential time, for which we have invented the clock. We can count and measure sequential time, and whilst this is useful, we can tend to miss the reality of our experience and lose our ability to act in a timely fashion. For acting we need timing. We need to explore the cyclic rhythmicity of time, and it is this which teaches us when and how to act.

Some of the other Greek terms for time give us further insight into decision making: Eon (αἰών), Eon or epoch is a period which is dominated by a particular pattern being an unchangeable feature of that period.

Timing and decision making is learning to walk, and knowing these times as they unfold in your life and your harmony with them is your wisdom. *Carpe diem* or seize the moment is the essence of timing and to master this you have to recognise that every moment is not pregnant with the same possibilities, and often when you miss the moment you have to wait through the interval or bend the interval in a way that favours a similar timing coming at you again.

In Arabic for instance, there are around 14 words for time, giving different windows into the phenomenon of time. For Phlegmatics decision making is about timing and curiosity as to the ways in which time may be viewed gives you a deeper appreciation of time and decisions. How many words do you think we have in English and what can they tell us about how we use our time?

Phlegmatic Communication

You know how to listen, and you really hear where people are. We would call your energy passive but don't misunderstand what that means. With regard to conversations passivity means that you know how to help others to talk to you. You invite the active into a space and make use of it by helping it to do what it would do naturally. Passivity is another way of acting, the active initiate and drive forward and the passive invite the active to initiate and encourage them to drive forward. Our civilisation prioritises the active and will tend to reward it. However, the passive possess overlooked secrets which, when understood, gives you access to other ways of getting things done. Water is passive and the roots of trees, animals and mankind must seek it to survive, the passive knows how to be sought, knows how to be needed and in return nurtures. Passivity is a power, it is not the absence of activity and it isn't a weakness; it is another power entirely.

Here is an example that may help, 'I remember being at school as a teenager in London and going to a Judo class. I was the skinniest in the class and a 200 lb+ punk rocker with a racist streak walks in, looks around the class, sets his eyes upon skinny me and smirks. I knew there would be trouble. He teams up with me and our Sensei smiled. I grew up in the Amazon and knew that there was no way that I could handle him with strength alone. It comes to our turn to be on the mat and he immediately attacks, and I let him. At this time I'm completely relaxed and he shakes me about like a rag doll and can't believe his luck. He swiftly throws me to the floor and sends his weight crashing down in order to crush me, but this is precisely what I wanted him to do, and he's done it! So, I break my fall and slip slightly to the side whilst opening my legs widely. He has now thrown himself between my two strongest limbs and I wrap him up like an anaconda but I've only got one chance at this because he is so strong. I squeeze hard and I feel his ribcage closing down. His bullish triumph changes to pain and terror and he realises that he's been had. He squeals in agony like a stuck pig.

Sensei intervenes and rescues him and with a glint in his eye says nothing about the illegality of the move. The bully looks at me incredulously, and of course, I look back at him as if I don't even know what happened. He gets up and he leaves, changes his clothing and never returns. This would be called a passive strategy and if his own weight had defeated him with no action from myself but a sidestep, then it would have been perfect. This was a passive in encouraging him to ensnare himself by being blinded by his own strength, then once he put himself squarely into the trap it is actively sprung. Often when facing Phlegmatic fighters, while you are playing checkers against their chess, you are left wondering if it had all been an accident.

Another example is the strategy of fruit trees, they produce fruits and we eat them for food, whilst all the plant wants to achieve is to spread its seeds. We eat the fruit and spread the seeds in the process. This is another form of passive strategy.

When we talk of Feminine and Passive energies, please do not assume them to be weak. They employ a level of strength that is not dependent upon strength and obvious power but upon subtle employment of your own nature for or against you. So in conversation you know how to listen and help people talk to you and you do not underestimate the power of the passive. Or, for that matter, of the feminine.

The problem often is that you listen to everyone and they all leave knowing very little about you. So many people just don't know how to listen. This can be a problem when building stable and healthy relationships. Yes, it inspires curiosity but sometimes you have to let the other person know and understand where you are coming from, and in this Cholerics are your natural teachers. They will let you know where and who they are in no uncertain terms. Remember that a relationship has give and take. And sometimes you need to leave a trail of breadcrumbs.

Making Your Needs Known and Understood

This is a weakness of yours for often the habit of empathising habituates you to neglect yourself. So that often your needs remain unknown and misunderstood. In relationships it is up to you to make your needs known and to ensure that your needs are understood. This allows you to make clear decisions about the sustainability of the relationship.

The Phlegmatic in Company

People drain you and it is an energetic transaction, therefore you need time alone to recover. This is a quality you share with Melancholics. Being in crowds and socialising drains you and you have to recover. In your case because of your intuitive and sensitive nature you can end up in empathy overload as your awareness of the emotional states of those around you is perpetual. It is easier if you are in a group and you have a clear intent and focus. However, you still need to decompress afterwards and prepare energically for these sessions. Don't underestimate the toll they take and or assume that this shouldn't happen, this is part of your constitutional makeup and you can't stop this from happening. You have to accept this as part of your life and acknowledge this and make space for it. Crowds and company will be one of your most difficult challenges, and the more exhausted you are the less energetic protection you will possess. Exhaustion will leave you wide open and vulnerable and so you should prepare yourself for these encounters.

4 Things Which Help Your Energetic Protection

1. Not facing people head on helps. If you angle your centre line away from their centre line this helps to limit the energetic exchange.

2. Fold your arms across your solar plexus to protect yourself from energetic onslaughts. Break the angle to increase the effectiveness.

3. Step back and keep your weight on the front foot, whilst doing the two above. This increases your protective energy. This would be similar to the Warrior Pose in Yoga, but executed to feel like a natural, everyday posture.

4. Remember that exhaustion leaves you more open to the energy of others and to feeling drained. Prepare by getting a good

night's rest if you can before being in company, and afterwards take a walk or sit alone to recover.

Remember that you require alone time and you don't have to justify yourself. This is just the way that you are wired, and there is no way that I know of to change this.

Silence

You require silence daily. You just need a period of this and you don't have to justify yourself in this to others. This is who you are and you require this. Once you've decompressed, your creative imagination will begin to roam and you need silence in order for this to take place. If you are stuck in crowded places you will begin to daydream to escape the crowd. This is completely natural and you don't need to think that this is abnormal. And instead of people around you criticising your daydreaming let them give you space and leave you alone. This is just the way that you're wired. Some things are accepted whether they make sense or not and they aren't going to change.

You'll get bored with people, so take time aside and though our culture assumes that extraversion and socialisation are always healthy, that doesn't make them right. For this one you need to trust your gut. You need silence and time alone and this is just how you are.

Ways to Decompress

Your arm has been twisted and now you find yourself stuck at a crowded event for the day. You start enthusiastically telling yourself that you've got this, and that it can't be that bad, and that you've done it before, and that others have been doing this since the dawn of mankind. Twenty blessed minutes into the day-long event an acquaintance turns up who intends to introduce you to everyone, saying, 'You won't be able to disappear into some secret corner like you always do!' That should have been your big red flag. The first hour goes by and you've listened to the life story of the 7th person. Won't they ever leave you alone? Then your lovely friend comes walking your way with yet another introduction! Yes, another one of those! Why are there so many people on earth? She introduces you to this guy who has been answering your emails (at work) for the last two years but you've never met and that could have continued until the end of the world. By now you're desperate and starting to feel trapped, hemmed in, and your heart rate is rising. He seems nice but you really need a break, so you excuse yourself and head for the toilet! You don't need the toilet and you don't wear makeup but you need an excuse, so you grab your friend's makeup bag and head for the bathroom, they told you that there was one on the third floor. That would be furthest away from everyone so you head that way to decompress. How on earth are you going to survive a whole day of this?

Now this has become a Mission Impossible, to find covert spaces or hide in the open without attracting attention.

5 First Steps

1. Scope the place out, and this is an excellent excuse. Tell them that you are going to explore, making it sound like an adventure. Scope the place out and find the cubby holes, hideouts and spaces that people will leave you alone in. Extend the exploration as this is your first break.

2. Set up your exit excuses, and if you need to, select a potential Phlegmatic or Melancholic companion, who will also need to make a getaway and with whom the mere exchange of a glance will be enough to communicate the desperation to escape.

3. Make sure that you've a book to read and things to do that absolutely have to be done when you need to invoke them.

4. Remember that a well meaning Sanguine and or a Choleric who has made you their social project are today's greatest problems. You need to lose them. Boring them to death loses Sanguines faster but Cholerics can be a lot more work.

5. Did you set up any rescuers? Rescuers are friends who know you well and understand your needs and so step in to rescue you with an excuse for you to decompress. If you don't find one, then this is going to be a tough day.

20 Ways to Make a Break For It With Excellent Excuses

1. I need to go to the toilet (this is no lie). You may not need to use the toilet but you do need to go.

2. Would you like something to drink? Go and find their drink the very long way around.

3. Could you point me in the direction of the kitchen?

4. Replace kitchen with any other location that works.

5. Can I help you with the service? (Yes volunteer).

6. Can I help you with (replace the service with anything that gets you some space).

7. Leave something in a safe place at one of the cubby holes or hiding places and remember it, so that you have to find it.

8. I have some material that I'm **obliged** to read.

9. Is there a quiet space for me to make a call? (This will get rid of almost everyone).

10. Download a 'fake a call' app. Just go to your phone app store and search for one and spend some time understanding the features. This is your nuclear option if you really need to get away. If it gets desperate then use it.

11. Just say that, 'I'm enjoying this conversation, but I'm not good with socialising and I need a break. Do you mind me coming back to continue the conversation later on in the day?' Make a note of where you ended the conversation and when you find them

later on start with your thoughts about what they had to say. That can be impressive and it shows that you were paying attention and were interested in what they had to say.

12. 'I need to relax a little, as it has been a tough period', and excuse yourself.

13. 'I'm an introvert and I can't handle lots of people for long periods of time. I really need a break.'

14. 'I've a document to read.' Now go and read that book.

15. 'I really need to make an important call.', then call a friend who knows you well, tell them hello, and that you hope that they are well and now you need to go and decompress.

16. 'Thanks for the conversation but I don't want to monopolise all your time.'

17. 'It's been great catching up with you! I've got to take care of something.'

18. 'Did you see where the toilets are?'

19. 'I have a question that I need to ask X, excuse me please.'

20. 'I need to check in with X. Thank you, it's been great chatting.'

21 Ways to Decompress

1. Return to one of those hidey holes: Yes that's why we located them for now in these places at intervals you may sit quietly for a few heavenly minutes.

2. Take walks around outside: Step outside and take deep breaths of fresh air and take your short walks. You've got to pace yourself through this social event.

3. Listen to the rain: Get some recordings of the rain on your phone and sit in a corner and listen to the rain. Just sit and listen.

4. Check your phone: Use your phone and catch up on your messages and keep an ebook or two that you can sit and read.

5. One-to-One conversations are easier: Find a person that you're comfortable with and have a more private and more intimate conversation. This can really help.

6. Head for the bar or buffet: Use the bar or buffet to focus on something in a way that gives you a socialisation break.

7. Read a book: find a corner and take out a book and even if you can't read just relax

and stare emptily at the words. It's meditative.

8. Find the pet: if the event has pets, spend some time with the pets and get to know them. This is deeply relaxing.

9. Sit and follow your breaths: find a corner and sit and concentrate on your breathing and relax. This is meditation.

10. Take photographs: photography allows you to engage with the event and maintain your personal space.

11. Listen to music: headphones and earbuds then listen to some music. Add following your breaths meditation if you really want deep decompression.

12. Visualise your favourite place: Phlegmatics know how to daydream and this is a superpower in these situations. Take time to head off to daydream in your favourite place.

13. Find or volunteer for a task: now that you've got the task, really get engrossed in it. Escape! Escape! Escape!

14. Get a drink or a snack: sit there with it for as long as you can enjoying it and being really engrossed in it. They call it

mindfulness but Phlegmatics have been doing this for millenia.

15. Find your companion: Remember that companion? Give them that furtive look and get away to decompress. Moaning about socialisation helps. It really does!

16. Find the quiet room: if they are really enlightened and have set up a quiet room then bless them! I don't need to tell you what to do!

17. Get outside and stretch: roll your shoulders especially and gently stretch. If you combine this with gentle deep breaths it releases tension and works wonders.

18. People watching: you're a Phlegmatic and this is something that you do every day. Sit quietly and observe the antics and see if you can predict what they will do next.

19. Get a notebook out: get a notebook out and journal, write poetry, doodle. Just do something and engross yourself whilst doing it.

20. Observe the decor: sit and meditatively take the decor in.

21. Plan your exit strategy: there can be nothing like the triumph of your final

escape, eh! Now sit down and daydream about it.

Finally, the day is over and you've survived! Well you won't be doing that again in a hurry, will you.

Don't Be Guilty About Being an Introvert

It takes all types to make the world and the fixation of our culture on the standards of extroverts with very little consideration for the needs of introverts is an insane position and it has consequences upon the psychological needs and health of introverts. Whilst the culture remains skewed in the direction of extroverts then we have to do what we do to secure our space. What we have to recognise is that it is up to introverts to let the world know about their needs and to call out gaslighting when it is done to protect extroverted standards. Let's keep calling it out and whilst we have to deal with it then have an arsenal in your pocket to deal effectively with this. Decompress in peace because you need it.

Presentations and Public Speaking

Yes, I know the very title is a source of terror. Since Phlegmatics hate being in the spotlight and prefer the sidelines this is almost the definition of hell. In work and as a student often presentations and or public speaking are unavoidable. The thing is that your discomfort with the spotlight is a reflex and so the discomfort is not at all an accurate prediction of the way that people will receive what you have to say. In fact, often when you have something to say people listen and this is because you are prone to make the most interesting observations. You are actually very interesting and the fact that your dislike of the limelight is a reflex, should tell you everything that you need to know. You're interesting but you don't like the space in which your interesting-ness is exposed to the world. The way that you feel about yourself and what you have to say is precisely the opposite of how people tend to receive what you have to say, and this is an opportunity to begin to narrow the gap between how you feel and how you're received and it is going to be a valuable but uncomfortable journey. What we can almost always guarantee is that you will make a valuable contribution to the world. You almost always nurture and that almost always makes the world better, so you were meant to struggle with this and this is a central pillar of your own personal development. Discomfort and growth are related and here you will really grow.

6 Reasons Why You Should Share Your Views and Insights

1. You are interesting and your insights usually matter. The only thing I can say in this case is, 'Get over yourself!'

2. When you speak to people you usually speak to where they are, by empathising with them. This is the essence of effective communication and you tend to do this naturally.

3. You spend a lot of time reflecting and creatively exploring and you think in ways that others often don't, so it is very likely that you will surprise them. Talk to them and keep surprising them and you do this naturally anyway.

4. Though you don't like the limelight you will have things to say and they will make a difference, don't you think that other Phlegmatics will benefit from seeing you shine? Won't it give them the courage to speak up? Well, you could just leave it all to the Cholerics, Melancholics and Sanguines! Just let them speak and dominate what you should do. Yes, you can easily spend your life just letting the Cholerics dominate! Wouldn't that be

wonderful? And you would only have yourself to blame! Yes, I agree with you! Why should Phlegmatics have a voice when Cholerics and Sanguines have so much to say?

5. Oh, and you know how so often you have to make the effort to find something interesting in what someone intent upon speaking to you has to say. Yes, I believe that you do! Well this could be your opportunity to inflict that on someone else! But because you are usually quite insightful, I doubt that this will happen.

6. There are times for silence, reflection and imagination and so there must be times for speech, presentation and sharing your insights. Wouldn't you agree that they are both necessary? Your comfort with one and discomfort with the other mirrors the Choleric difficulties, don't you think? They have their challenges and here is yours. You don't have to rise to the challenge but you will have to deal with the consequences, so why don't you choose the most pregnant of the challenges? (I'm enjoying watching you squirm! Yes! I see you!)

I call this the squirm space and it is the space in which incredible growth and changes happen. Good luck!

16 Ways Phlegmatics Can Motivate Themselves For Public Speaking

Ok, so now you've finally realised that you have to do it and if you've never confronted the dark shadow of terror, by now you probably have, and if you've never sensed its approach? Well, now you have. Here are 15 ways to motivate yourself for the task.

1. Daydream about success: Visualise yourself delivering the speech, standing tall and confidently banishing the dark smoky tendrils of failure from the room. The gentle light of your presence and what you have to say reaches the hearts of people and they receive what you have to say. Afterwards, they tell you all of the amazing things you want to hear them say about your speech or presentation. Then see yourself sitting quietly in the corner, alone and happy that you actually did it.

2. Prepare! Prepare! And Prepare: It doesn't matter how anxious you feel, let yourself know that you're putting the work in.

Practise, and if you are worried about freezing up when you get onto the podium, then practise some more. Know your speech and presentation thoroughly. Knowing that you are putting the work in reduces the anxiety. You will feel fear and that is a good thing.

3. Practise regularly and find the rhythm: Your speech or presentation has its internal rhythm, and practising helps you find its flow. Once you learn how to find its flow, you will become more comfortable and you will know the internal structure of your content.

4. Practise regularly with larger and larger audiences: As you prepare first practise alone, then in front those close to you, then the wider circle of family and friends. Then colleagues and those you can trust to give you valuable feedback. Get comfortable with their reactions and accept both praise and criticism. And remember that you will be the one to decide which criticisms and praise you will act upon.

5. Focus on delivering your message: You have something incredible to say, so focus on saying it, don't make it about you,

serve the message and its delivery to your audience. See the problems you're solving go away and serve the process. It's about the message and not about you.

6. You're preparing: Say it, repeat it. 'I am prepared!'. Tell yourself about your message and why it's important that people get it.

7. Build your victory: Break your public speaking project and its goals into small manageable steps that you can win. Make winning easy, don't make it hard and celebrate your wins.

8. Turn your audience into friends: Let your message befriend your audience and imagine them as your friends, who are absolutely committed to your success and are interested in what you have to say.

9. Develop a pre-presentation routine: keep yourself relaxed, warm and connected. Breathe deeply, stretch, listen to some music, be gently prepared and know your routine inside out. Be so comfortable with your routine that you don't have to think about it.

10. Look at others deliver successful speeches: Now model, imitate and learn

their techniques. Find speakers that inspire you and get downright geeky about watching their artistry.

11. Practice with those who practise: go into training if you can and practise with others who are practising. Share your knowledge and technique and encourage each other.

12. Use this as an opportunity to grow: Yes you don't like this but this is part of your personal development and use it to grow and become more rounded.

13. It doesn't have to be perfect: Perfection is overrated, focus on small regular improvements and accept the imperfections. It is ok. Just commit to small regular improvements and let the journey begin.

14. Focus on your breath: Breathe as you speak and keep yourself grounded, with even breaths. You will be surprised at how well this will make you feel and how much it calms your anxieties and fears.

15. Plan rewards: When you do well, particularly well, reward yourself.

16. Look at yourself in the mirror: Look at yourself straight in the eye in the mirror

and tell yourself how well you are doing. Be grateful for your successes.

Why Dealing With Crowds is Important

Company! Oh no! Oh yes, to the sidelines and observing! Being the focus is not the strength of the Phlegmatic but there is great benefit in mastering your journey through crowds. Yes they drain you and there is a little that you can do about that, but they will remain draining. You have to take them in smaller doses and think about them as a homoeopathic principle. The homoeopathic principle treats the disease with the principle that causes the disease in such small traces that the life force, having sensed the thing, responds to repel it. It is a way of teasing the life force's defensive responses out into open activity as a healing principle, that the homoeopath guides. You can use crowds to do this and to develop your capacity to explore and consciously employ these aspects of yourself. Yes, there are sides of you that you like and sides that you will like less, but you have to embrace you as your whole self and see the appropriateness of these different aspects of yourself. To be able to muster these diverse aspects of yourself appropriately is mastery. View dealing with crowds as your opportunity to meet those often hidden aspects of yourself and learn to employ them appropriately.

You see crowds become your servant. A servant that you may be reflexively wary of, but in order for your treatment of them to be just, you must pay attention to their qualities. Understanding their strengths, weaknesses and quirks will ensure that you know when there are jobs that they are uniquely suited to and rather than just allowing your biases to dictate your behaviour, you would have to acknowledge your biases and find the internal space to grant them their place, without being dominated inappropriately by them. Yes, we all have biases and they don't make us bad, many of them we inherit from our socialisation. What is problematic is when we don't acknowledge them and ensure that we get ahead of them to make sure that we are not blinded by them. Then you have the opportunity to do the deep work of self interrogation. But this book is not about that.

I'm saying that you will be quite biased about aspects of your own self, but they are part of you and you have to begin to see them beyond your biases, which pre-package your responses and bind you into blind courses of action. The discomfort of crowds will tease aspects of you in a most revealing manner. But don't just overwhelm yourself with them, be homoeopathic about it and hold the space to see how your responses come bubbling to the surface.

8 Uses of Crowds

1. You've got conflict resolution skills: your natural dislike of conflict has led you to develop excellent conflict avoidance skills. You've also an excellent disposition for conflict resolution. In crowds conflict and arguments naturally arise and you often can't escape. You will have to deal with the mounting impulse to escape and remain calm (you are good at that). Inevitably there will be times when people will ask you to decide on disagreements between them or just for your opinion and here is where you should practise your conflict resolution skills by getting each part to see where the other may be coming from and if possible you may resolve the disagreement but you don't have to. You can get them to empathise with each other and continue watching the entertaining social experiment.

2. People watching: hone your skills and find the spaces in crowds where conflict

will arise and who will initiate it and find the places where harmony and cooperation abides and who maintains it. Now, once you've learned to do this then place yourself in each group at intervals. Study the dynamics of these situations and what they inspire in you.

3. Learn to deal with your natural wariness of crowds: we all have an autonomic nervous system and autonomic responses. Yours is set to protect you from the attention of crowds whilst a Sanguine's is set to seek them out. Do you see the difference? Observe your own dislike, the pattern of emotional responses and the narratives which attach themselves to these feelings in order to get you out of the space. Now you are aware of them, breathe deeply and observe them. Next you will learn to deal with them.

4. Learn to deal with your automatic protective responses against crowds: this is a natural and necessary reaction but it should be appropriately employed. Because socialisation is a necessary part of the life of social creatures, this is something that you need to learn to

manage. Ok! Now that you've finished squirming here are some suggestions:

1. Whilst you are experiencing these thought cascades and sensations, push your feet into the ground so that you really feel the soles of your feet.

2. Now relax and breathe deeply so that you experience your breath sinking into the soles of your feet, and press your tongue gently against the roof of your mouth. Does this make you feel more grounded?

3. Stand back in yourself, fill your body up with yourself and feel the soles of your feet and your back.

4. Let your breath be smooth, deep, continuous and the in-breaths are longer than the out-breaths.

5. Watch an argument or disagreement and say nothing, but track the feelings and thought cascades in yourself. Interesting, eh?

6. Find a safe corner and sit safely there and watch the crowd. Now track the feelings

and thought cascades in yourself. Once again, interesting, eh?

7. Mastering empathy-overwhelm: practising looking away when you notice how people are feeling, see it but don't see it and visualise yourself in a giant balloon, like some great womb protecting you from all the energies flowing in. Look from behind the walls of this great womb and push and poke the flexible wet and strong durable nurturing walls.

8. Dealing with Social Anxiety: well, you don't need anyone else to convince you that this is a thing. Use the great womb to help you to build up your capacity to deal with this aspect of your response over time. Return to item 4 to integrate more tools to improve your capacity to deal with your social anxieties. You'll start to enjoy the challenge with time.

9. Mastering social interactions: use crowds to learn how to effortlessly start and finish conversations. Learn to slip away unnoticed, and deeply understand how to negotiate this social space. This will do more than anything else to reduce social anxiety.

Phlegmatic Choosing a Profession

> "One's profession is not just a way of earning a living; it is a way of giving form and content to one's life and of contributing to the community."
>
> **-- Truth and Method, Hans Georg Gadamer**

This is the central challenge of the Phlegmatic seeking a profession. They will often be shy to state their challenge clearly but this is the Phlegmatic challenge. And the question can be stated thus, 'Is this professional life path that I am considering worth receiving the content of my life, and does it contribute and make a difference to my community?

No, you don't like stress, you avoid conflict, you don't like change, you love staying in your comfort zone, you tend to underestimate the skills you have, you don't like self promotion, you fear failure, you don't like activity unless you have to, you prefer observation to action, you don't like asserting yourself, you procrastinate because you spend so much energy interrogating your course of action and you aren't the natural networker. It had better really be worth the effort because you will have to climb these mountains. So take your time to choose and whilst you choose, acquire the necessary core skills to make it easier to commit to your chosen direction.

I Want to Make a Difference to the World

Phlegmatics really want to make a difference to the world but does the world really want to change? They want people to be understood with empathy but will it ever make a difference. They think about lots of things but will people ever care? If people understood these issues the world would be a very different place but would they really understand and will the world really change? The Phlegmatic listens to you and can see your way out but won't tell you because will it really make a difference? There is a deep pessimistic impulse present in the Phlegmatic psyche. This pessimistic impulse gives shape to much of the narrative, emotional landscape and deep Phlegmatic fears. They often don't do anything about this because it won't really change anything.

When a Phlegmatic chooses a life path it really must have meaning for them because of their tendency to investigate rigorously and to regularly interrogate whether what they want

89

to do should be done. Whatever life path they choose will have to stand up to regular and thorough scrutiny, so they need to choose carefully and over time. If the affirmative answer keeps coming back to them, then the lifepath begins to assert a claim upon them, and that claim has to grow its roots. Because of this it is perhaps important for the Phlegmatic to ensure that they at least have a solid foundation in some area that allows flexibility.

Because the Phlegmatic requires a journey to become aware and clear about the contents of the depths of their own mind and their professional passions, they cannot demand of themselves that they should be clear about the direction of their professional lives in some decision taken when they were 17 years old. That would in most cases be an oppression. The Phlegmatic nature requires that there is a passionate connection to what they do or they will experience what they are doing as a form of imprisonment.

If you are a phlegmatic and making such a journey, then give yourself time and trust the process. Here is what you can be sure of, it will involve nurturing, service and listening. Phlegmatics are capable of finding unexpected niches and infusing these qualities into so many professions. Yes, you want to make a difference but to do so you usually have to, 'Make haste slowly!' as the Russian proverb says.

Trust that you will find your niche and patiently but steadily set out in the certainty that you will find it. When you find it, the chances are that it will scare you but the claim on you will be such that you realise that you don't really have a choice.

Apprehension

Apprehension will accompany you on this journey. Apprehension and discomfort are your friends. You want to do something that makes a difference but you fear being seen. Fear of failure. Fear that you're not good enough. Anxiety that people will not recognise you. Fear that you will be successful. Fear of how success will come. Anxiety that it will not come. Fear of fear. Fear of not having enough fear. Fear of having too much fear. Give fear its place and let it be there, don't fight fear, for it only becomes bigger than it actually is. Accept fear, give it its place and accept that it is your companion on your journey and that it cannot dictate what you do.

What you do has to be big enough to displace your fears. It has to be so important to you that you must overcome your fears. This is your hero's journey, your monsters are within your breast and you must slay them but for this to happen the quest must be greater than your fears.

Beware of those things with which you seek to distract yourself from what lays its claims upon your life energy and path. They will usually involve a sensuous aspect for only they may momentarily obscure the pull of your path. They offer momentary, fleeting, spellbinding preoccupation, but once they are done, the void and emptiness come rushing back in. When you find yourself here, know that you are already in battle with your dragon and if you do not commit to the fight then it will not end well.

Your life path battle and journey is the timeless challenge of the Phlegmatic. Your Elemental Waters were created for this journey. Proceed!

Creativity

Your being requires creativity and the essence of creativity is the jump off the cliff of the comfortable into the space where the emergent emerges. True creativity requires risk. You get it wrong. It doesn't work. You've wasted the ingredients. They may not like it. And if they like it, can I make it again?

And here is your challenge: you require safety but even more than safety you require creativity. Phlegmatics are deep wells. Perhaps deeper than any other type. Your fulfilment requires creativity but you also need safety. Have one and you lose the other and have the other and you lose the one. The life challenge of the Phlegmatic is the freedom to creatively step beyond their fears.

Accept the terror of the immense nature with which the Phlegmatic has been blessed, without ever asking for it or even desiring it. You have this depth, subtle intelligence and vastness and you have the need for safety, whilst the only way out is across the tightrope.

The Phlegmatic challenge is to willingly commit to walk the tightrope and for Phlegmatics life will perpetually remind you of your primal challenge.

Phlegmatic Friend

As a Phlegmatic friend you are the best. You are loyal, unbelievably supportive, empathetic, understanding, dependable, calming, kind and compassionate, boundlessly diplomatic, unbelievably discrete, you listen and you keep secrets secure, your humility is beautiful, your generosity astounds us, you promote an atmosphere of harmony, you forgive boundlessly and you know how to maintain friendships across the years. In short you are a steadfast, affectionate and nurturing friend.

You are really selective about who you let into your circle and you will just refuse to engage with someone who you don't want. However your sense of compassion, harmony and forgiveness often make you break this rule against your better intuition because after they have persisted and stuck around, then your compassion and kindness tend to get the better of you and usually your initial feelings are proven right. I'll leave you to work that one out but this is a consistent pattern across Phlegmatics. If you are one of those people who get past the Phlegmatic defences and finally get them to let you in, then you would do well to examine yourself, for they have very likely seen something and it isn't good. One of the great difficulties of relationships with Phlegmatics is that they see through you clearly, with piercing intuition. That is the price that you will pay for this relationship and if you are really close and trusted, they will tell you things about yourself with a diplomacy and subtlety that requires your attention, or you will just miss it. The Phlegmatic need to avoid confrontation and promote harmony, means that they will always strive to tell you things in a manner that doesn't upset you.

As a phlegmatic you must have and maintain boundaries, for often, more invasive types take your gentle nature for weakness and will serially overstep the mark. You have to stand up to Cholerics, they respect nothing else, Sanguines will attempt to overwhelm you and you have to deflect them and they will be so often so caught up with the energy of their approach that they don't notice as they overfly the mission objective (yes you can use wind against wind), Melancholics will attempt to batter you into submission with logic, you can give Melancholics a one word answer that throws them into a logical iterative tailspin as they can't help themselves from silently deconstructing their own argument (they really cannot help themselves). If not, you just have to refuse to hear them out. Everyone is right from their own perspective and you, Phlegmatic, are no different. You need those boundaries for water needs its container, passive power gathers at a dam, and waterfalls happen where the river narrows and falls precipitously in height, the power in water is by its boundaries. You must understand your considerable power in relationships (and I know you hate thinking about it like this) and you must understand that whether you choose to wield it consciously or not, you will wield it, and in order to wield it in ways that bring harmony and growth to everyone, you must submit to wisdom, so grow your natural wisdom and challenge yourself.

If your relationships are all only comfortable and secure then what will you learn? The stone in the shoe makes you imagine a better shoe. Why do you think that you have been blessed with such patience and tolerance?

In friendships, ensure that they appreciate your humility and do not mistake it for weakness. This is a certain sign of stupidity of a dangerous and exploitative kind. If they don't appreciate what you bring then help them to go find something else that they can appreciate more, and when they come back to complain about the most esteemed and appreciated prizes, remind them that this is what they sought and that they should learn to have 'gratitude' for the immense gifts that they have been given. Do not allow people to empty their bucket loads into yours just because you listen. Your listening is the privilege of a few. Why? Because you can't handle listening to too many. Treat apples like apples and don't expect them to do the job of coconuts.

Oh, and you are so committed to your dislike of change, that you anxiously commit so much activity to keeping things the same, the world is in change whilst things stay the same. Wisdom is to understand how to work with the change that must happen and maintain the fundamentals that just stay the same, if you are working too hard then you've missed the point. This leads to so much procrastination, over-accommodation and clinging to dying comfort zones.

> "The Tao never does, yet through
> it all things are done."
> **– Tao Te Ching, Chapter 37**

Do you see why you have to submit to the flows of wisdom in all things, Phlegmatic? Remember that it is in relationships that emotional and psychological imbalance and harm are born. Mastering relationships and relating is the skill most suited to you, it is unbelievably hard work, boundlessly rewarding and for you there is nothing as fulfilling as a harmonious relationship.

> "Holding together brings good fortune. Inquire of the oracle once again whether you possess sublimity, constancy, and perseverance; then there is no blame. Those who are uncertain

> gradually join. Whoever comes
> too late meets with misfortune."
> **-- I-Ching, Hexagram 8 - Bi (Holding Together)**

This quote from the I-Ching shows the essence of your role, you hold together harmoniously, and this itself brings good fortune. Sublimity, constancy and (gentle) perseverance are your qualities. Your company nurtures and the cultures you engender, nurture. This is a quiet, gentle power and sensible people see it. Those deprived of this are unfortunate. In all humility you must recognise that your close company when you fulfil the best of your Phlegmatic qualities and commit to the work of growing as a Phlegmatic, is an honour and brings immense benefits to those who join. And if you choose to flow like a river or stay stagnant like a swamp then just study these forms of Elemental Water to see the results.

Phlegmatic in Love

The Phlegmatic in love draws the one they love into a spider's web of kindness. They listen, they nurture and they are quietly generous. The pursuer, however, must proceed carefully for the Phlegmatic will withdraw and become inaccessible. Loud noises, sharp abrasive movements and pushy people don't really work for Phlegmatics. They love deeply and their loyal nature means that they expect loyalty and deep love. However, they require reassurance and are almost certain that it won't last. You have to keep turning up. Where Sanguines give their whole hearts, Cholerics make it blatantly clear and claim you, the Phlegmatic needs you to commit to your slow, gentle, steady chase. They assume that little gestures of affection carry large meanings because that is how it is for the Phlegmatic.

Phlegmatic, if you are being pursued by a Choleric or a Melancholic, remember that your small gestures may be missed for very different reasons, Cholerics make big gestures and so notice bigger gestures, whilst Melancholics will just be unsure. As for the special case of the Sanguine, they are so certain of their beauty and desirability that they cannot conceive of someone not liking them. As far as the Sanguine is concerned, the night, the stars, the sun and the moon are all in love with them. In comparison to the Phlegmatic uncertainty this may seem insane but people are people and this is just how we are wired. Where with the Choleric you have to stick your hand in the lion's mouth and accept your bites to win their heart, with the Phlegmatic, patience, constancy and dependability are your assets. Yes, they may be attracted to some danger but they have to know that you will be there without them having to pursue you.

When you are clearly a safe person to love, the Phlegmatic becomes quite romantic but they really need their space. You need to acknowledge and honour this need or they will become imbalanced and even sick. Please honour their boundaries. They are imaginative and once they accept you in, you will be exposed to their sharp wit. And if they begin to tease you then you are quite likely in. Where a Choleric boundary is like a wall the Phlegmatic boundary is like a moat and once you're in the castle you're in. They don't look forward to all that painful uncertainty in a hurry and they are very forgiving, but be careful because once they disconnect, it is quite likely over and it is incredibly difficult to rescue the relationship.

Remember that the Phlegmatic that feels safe and comfortable tends to be an imaginative lover.

The World According to the Phlegmatic

> Birotteau was fundamentally a
> man of order and routine; he

lived peacefully in the domestic sphere, never seeking to challenge the status quo or indulge in speculative ventures. His gentle and accommodating nature endeared him to those around him, as he preferred to maintain harmony rather than provoke conflict.

César Birotteau - Honoré de Balzac

Well Birotteau may have been a man of order and routine but in his active internal world there will be many things that he will consider and question, however because he values harmony, safety and stability, much of this will remain unexpressed in favour of stability and this is why Phlegmatics absolutely need a creative output within which it is possible to express this unexpressed roving and exploratory aspect. Yes, Phlegmatic, you must have a creative activity if you are to be balanced and healthy.

CV

I observe my world and prefer to let things do themselves, rather than wasting my time rushing from place to place like a headless chicken trying to get things done that would happen by themselves anyway, or to dedicate my life to making happen that which stops happening as soon as I stop. I prefer to work with things rather than against them. I therefore value action and behaviour based upon wisdom, constancy and intelligence. I let things get things done and help them to complete themselves. I avoid the foolish and kick myself if they drag me into their dramas. You might think that I am lazy, but I really don't care very much. At least not enough to be forced to change my way of doing things. I prefer it when a little action has profound long lasting results. If I don't want to engage with you, good luck to you!

I'm not goal-oriented and I love the journey rather than being focused upon the goal exclusively. I trust that I will arrive and want to do so elegantly, gently and smoothly. I think or rather feel things through and I do this quietly. I will listen to you and respect you for listening to me. Of course I take a long time to work out what I want to say but everyone is different. When I ask questions I would advise you to consider your answers because I will play what you have said over and over in my head as I seek to penetrate beneath the surface of what you said.

Empathy and forgiveness are at my core, they aren't really even a choice. So I will tend to forgive often and often understand why you do things, but my pragmatic nature dictates that I will draw conclusions about you based upon what you have done. If by chance I comment on this and you don't like what you hear, know that I have watched you for a very long time, have supplied you with many excuses and am now quite certain of how you are, shortcomings and all.

If I focus upon winning I want this to be done with elegance and I will tend to have spent time and many repetitions refining the technique. If I really get into winning it will be in the manner of mastery and as always I will tend to be humble but don't be surprised if I don't share my techniques with you. I have to respect you, love you and really admire your dedication to do so. It is hard work for me so I'd prefer not to do it but I will if you are exceptional.

I am incredibly diplomatic and have excellent people skills but that doesn't mean that I am always comfortable with people and company. I need lots of space and breaks thank you.

Things I Hate

Loud people, stupid people, disloyal people, people trying to rush me, arrogant people and the limelight. Yes, it tends to have something to do with people! Don't talk too much, don't lack a sense of humour, and don't push yourself into my space when I don't want you to be there. I love flexibility and love routine and so hate imposed flexibility and hate imposed routine. Yeah! Work that one out, it must be about imposing, what do you think? I'm not intimidated by silence and hate people talking too much and especially inappropriately. I fear losing people and so hate the fact that they may walk away but I can live with it.

My Outlook

I'll spend my life looking on at the drama that is life and the entertaining antics of others. I don't have a problem doing nothing because I am doing so much inside.

The Phlegmatic According to the Rest of the World

The Good Points

You are quiet, loyal, observant companions and we ignore your insights at our own peril. Your nurturing nature means that you look after those close to you. You give the most insightful and incredible advice and it is rarely wrong. Your diplomacy is first rate and your diplomatic advice masterful. You always consider the feelings of everyone and we can only imagine how tiring that must be.

Your company is slow paced, restoring and you listen attentively. If we can get you to speak it is always fascinating but we have to give you lots of time and the silences may seem really long to hot types. Like the Choleric, when you break off a relationship there is very little chance of return as you have given them more chances than you think they deserve and so severance after serial forgiveness is often final.

You are unbelievably considerate.

Supporting you is often difficult because so much goes on beneath the surface! When it works it works but when you change sometimes the reasons are too subtle for you to explain but it took us a while to work this out. Oh, and you procrastinate so much and are so often unbelievably indecisive. But then there are types of decisions which you seem to take deep inside of you and with them you are utterly immovable.

The Complaints

We can spend a lifetime with you and know nothing about you save what you wish to share. You can stay silent until silence is ominous. Yes, if we wish to be your close friend then we have to embrace silence. And you will listen and listen, work it all out and take action like a hermetically sealed vessel. You will remain expressionless and it has all gone on beneath the surface and we are none the wiser save by the proof of your actions.

Oh, and how you underestimate yourself, play yourself down, doubt yourself and avoid the limelight when it is you that they should be listening to. This one makes us want to strangle you, but we've given up trying to convince you otherwise.

You slip away and avoid and we can't get a handhold on you to get you back. If we can accuse you of being unreliable it is because of this.

Ah, and your self-righteousness is connected to your empathy. But I don't really want to talk about this one.

Spot The Phlegmatic

"You can tell a Phlegmatic by their relaxed, easy going attitude. They are usually not in a hurry and take life at a slow and easy pace. They do not force things along and do not like to be forced. Their usual method of dealing with a person intent upon forcing them along, is to slow down, pretend not to understand, or to subtly and calmly sabotage the project.

They will observe for long periods of time, as they seek to perceive the deeper movements, motivations, sequences and cycles that shape things. They relax and harmonise with things as they seek to perceive what a thing is and how it is. Whereas the Melancholic is interested in the why and how, the Phlegmatic is interested in the what and how.

Phlegmatics will not engage if they do not want to and will look on with mild but imperceptible amusement at the activity of those engaged in whatever changing pursuits the other temperaments may be engaged in. Why rush, they may say, take your time and experience life, things and situations. They tend to have a wry, intelligent wit, that speaks volumes as to the depth of their intelligence and are able to get under the skin of all the temperaments with their occasional pointed observations.

Whilst the Sanguine's emotional intelligence is manifested in their interaction, that of the Phlegmatic manifests in their subtleness of observation and uncanny knack for empathy."

Know Yourself, Alex Carberry

Summary

We are at the end of the journey through the hidden treasure of the pure Phlegmatic. You would miss them whilst they are in full view and I hope this exploration has given an insight into the absolute treasures that may hide whilst standing right before you. You certainly will have gained some insights and I hope this better equips you to navigate your relationships with them and if you are blessed to be a Phlegmatic, then I hope that this has given you deeper insight into the currents sweeping through your depths and briefly coming to the surface before plunging below again.

This type easily possesses wisdom and their challenge is to find the balance in facing their fears with appearing socially active in the world. Yes, you have weaknesses but you of all people understand the strengths of your weaknesses. Your need for reassurance, your fears and your doubts are necessary but they cannot dictate how you act if you are to find balance.

You are of the Elemental Water and so conceal the deep currents flowing in the deepest depths within. I wish you success and the pleasure of swimming and diving within and the victory of plunging out into the world with a courage that the Phlegmatic must learn to find. I left the secrets to this one in the book if you can find them.

Now to the mixes!

The Mixes

Introduction

The Phlegmatic expresses Elemental Water, flexibility, spreading, imperceptibility, subtlety, seeking the low and cooling. This adaptable element which penetrates earth, rendering it pliable, cools fire and puts it out or is heated into steam or is evaporated into air, cooling it and causing it to return its water to the Earth. This is the element of cycles, flexibility and life. The Qur'an says:

> Are the disbelievers not aware that the heavens and the earth used to be joined together and that We ripped them apart, that We made every living thing from water? Will they not believe?
> **Al Qur'an 21:30**

Water is inextricably linked to life and we see that Phlegmatics nurture and that where there is water we find life. In Ayurveda we find that the *Kapha* includes the drier and earthier types as well as the watery ones. This is the wet of the *Kapha* and with heat it heads into the *Vata*. For the alchemical intermingling of the Elements of Air, Fire and Earth, very different qualities are brought forth. However, with Elemental Water as the base there is an even stability, connectivity and fusion.

Elemental Water is the first Element to emerge in the cosmological picture, the cycle is Water - Air - Fire - Earth, and in the coolness of Earth the Elemental Water regathers and the cycle begins again. Water is always the closest in emergence to the fundamental undifferentiated realm which we may sometimes refer to as the Abyss or *Ahadiyya*, meaning the realm of Absolute Oneness or Unicity. Elemental Water would cover a continuum from the emergence of Aether to the manifestation of Elemental Water, so that it is the first Elemental form and the most undifferentiated and as such the foundation from which all the other Elemental forms arise, it is as if they are hidden in water. So that Water is close to the Divine Tablet in nature and allows the inscription of forms upon it; it responds to the subtlest energetic forms as if being inscribed upon by The Pen. If you would like to see more on this look specifically at the sections on The Mixes in Know Yourself Choleric and Know Yourself Melancholic.

There are sciences in all of the traditional medicines for the inscribing of energetic medicine upon water. This is employed in homoeopathy and there is a developed science of imprinting prescriptions of Qur'anic verses upon water to be used as medicine. It may also be inscribed upon Earth as in the inscription of verses on the insides of a silver vessel and the drinking of water poured from it. Water is the most flexible solvent in Modern Chemistry, not to speak of Alchemy.

In the body, blood and lymphatic fluids are the water and in cases of chronic dehydration, limited blood volume causes the heart and hormonal systems to overwork, which is seen as unleashing excess fire, which leads to the depositing of earth; constipation, thickening of lymphatic fluids, prostate build up, kidney stones and the disorder of our mineral balance. This energetic picture often tells us where to look so that we can investigate and is not as simplistic as modern thinkers often assume in their arrogant underestimations of the intelligence of pre-modern thinkers.

Elemental Water is the Energy which connects the parts and holds them together (as solvents and suspensions do). Because it is connected to the Abyss it has profound connections to the world of intuition, in which knowledge reaches you whole and undifferentiated. The dream world is connected to water and the seas, and so water binds life, intuition and spirit.

It is perhaps for this reason that intuition must be employed with pure intent, for like water it becomes murky or clear with the energy of intent.

Phlegmatics will often struggle to bring forth a language to articulate their intuitive insights and for this reason an artistic expression begins to give them the skills, language and ability to give expression to these insights. With Phlegmatics, creative expression is a necessary component of their lives and the habit of visiting this aspect of the psychological and creative underbelly of our being provides a discipline that is needed to unfold this aspect of ourselves. Remember that water is fundamentally creative and that without water there is no life. Phlegmatics must learn to swim in the deep waters within themselves, which they very quickly discover, stretch beyond them. The separation of Order and Chaos is meaningless for the Phlegmatic for they see that Chaos always has its internal order and that any order which is not based upon this Chaotic internal order is perishing. Where the Melancholic sees Order and has to struggle with Chaos, the Phlegmatic sees and trusts the patterned order in everything. Like Elemental Water the Phlegmatic has a unified vision of reality and may adopt the language of opposites but in fact, easily discerns the unity underlying all things.

The Phlegmatic expresses the Feminine Archetype in the potentialities of The Cold and The Wet, expressing humility and seeking obscurity, qualities that the Sufis love. However, since Elemental Water dominates the Kidneys as a functional organ, Phlegmatics hold memory, fear and see into the past and the present. They are criticised as having very little ambition but this is not the complete story, their imagination grasps the present with flashes into the future and they are not dominated by the world of illusion in which we construct and enslave ourselves to desirable futures. Water is the basis of life and in the Divine dance of love the Phlegmatics are already content.

There are Three bio-types within the Phlegmatic species:

Phlegmatic-Sanguine

Phlegmatic-Choleric

and Phlegmatic-Melancholic.

Each expresses very different Phlegmatic possibilities. And you will always be able to recognise the Phlegmatic within these types. Two of these types give access to Active Archetype strategies and energies, whilst the Phlegmatic-Melancholic which is double cool, outwardly ends up with an unbelievably active psychological, problem solving and imagining nature.

The Phlegmatic Forest

The differences between Phlegmatic types is understood by delving into how the servant aspect of the temperamental mix affects the manner in which the Phlegmatic is expressed. The Phlegmatic master in their temperamental mix makes use of the servant or secondary type. The Sanguine of the Phlegmatic-Sanguine gives the Phlegmatic access to Sanguine strategies and qualities; the Choleric of the Phlegmatic-Choleric provides access to the Choleric; and the Melancholic in the Phlegmatic-Melancholic combination lends access to the Melancholic. In the Know Yourself Method we consider the base the master temperament and the servant which is the next dominant temperament which is in service to the master temperament. We do this because these will outline the broad foundations of your type, allowing you to study yourself in manageable detail. As you become more familiar with the dynamics of your own inner workings you will begin to understand how the other elements express themselves in you. You will also begin to grasp how different circumstances affect your psychological and physical health.

Phlegmatic-Sanguine: The Phlegmatic provides the base and the Sanguine traits serve the Phlegmatic impulses. This is a complementary mix, meaning that the behaviour of the types is consistent as the two types mix well.

Phlegmatic-Choleric: The Phlegmatic provides the base and the Choleric traits serve the Phlegmatic impulses. This is a non-complementary mix. This type can become quite Sanguine when they are comfortable and healthy, whilst at the same time being generally choleric, especially when well.

Phlegmatic-Melancholic: The Phlegmatic provides the base and the Melancholic traits serve the Phlegmatic impulses. This is a cool type, with a vast active inner life, with very little visible evidence of this activity. This is quite deceptive.

The Phlegmatic-Sanguine

Give me my space, and let me be. I am water and wind, the calm exterior stands as I slip and twist through the fingers of those who would pin me down. I am an incredibly diplomatic Phlegmatic and Phlegmatics are already diplomatic. Being contained will kill me. I need to flow like water and be as free as the wind. The strategies of the phlegmatic and the sanguine are smoothly and consistently combined within me.

I love my space and like to observe from the sidelines, and do not like to be trapped as the centre of attention.

The World According to the Phlegmatic Sanguine

I'm hyper-flexible, accommodating and need to keep my options open.

My waters lead the wind. I stand aside and observe like a Phlegmatic with a flair for the diplomatic, and prefer to dart in and withdraw to a safe space on the sidelines outside of the limelight. Often my diplomatic and people skills successes bring people crowding into my space and this doesn't work for me. I need to be able to come and go as it suits me. Pinning me down and restricting my ability to come and go doesn't work for me and leaves me feeling trapped, exhausted and desperate. Yes I enjoy the company and conversation when I choose, but I have to be very comfortable with you. The flowing nature of both water and wind, means that I am elegant, graceful and unassuming. Whereas Sanguines need to dominate the limelight, I am a Sanguine that avoids it. I work best hidden and then gently come onto the scene to do what I have to and then I fade into the background. I have to be able to flow and so suffer terribly from a lack of boundaries, which I absolutely need to be healthy. This is my achilles heel and if you are my friend or companion, you would do well to protect this for me without forcing it upon me. It is better to give me time to recognise the benefits that you bring rather than trying to enforce them upon me in a hurry. You have to take your time.

I observe and observe and observe and give very little expression to what I have seen, my actions however speak my conclusions and direction. You have to give me lots of time to articulate my thoughts and often I will take a long time to start, waters are deep and though I have a Sanguine aspect, first I have to dive deep in to find those pearls and bring them to the surface. As a result I'm the Sanguine that doesn't say the first thing that comes to my mind and I don't put my foot in it.

I feel my way to solutions and have a genius for working with people, and so will tend to build in gradual layers and it is more that I grow and tend a solution than imposing it upon the situation. So when I build a solution they tend to be robust, well thought out and repeatedly tested. They are robust not because I think of every eventuality but because I build gradually, observe the results and see what else is needed. The goal oriented may find this difficult because whilst they need a great overarching theory to drive towards, I trust what is truly there, find it and bring it gradually to fruition and because I am a Phlegmatic at base I need clarity so that it emerges clearly.

I nurture my way through social relations, and whilst my cousin the Sanguine-Phlegmatic loves connecting people, I would rather nurture them and provide a good environment for them to connect. My goal is to nurture and so I tend to make sacrifices. If you are my companion or friend you will need to keep an eye on this and remind me, because for the waters to pour forth they must be replenished.

Intuitive insight is my superpower, and I will drift past the obvious to dwell in the depths, for the obvious emerges from the depths, yes, the impulse root speaks the reality of the behaviour, so yes, I prefer to focus upon the depths, and need silence whilst I explore and dwell there. The motivations reveal the entire pattern. So where the dry may have goals, I find the significant points on the journey and sail my ship through them. Yes, the journey is much more interesting than being dominated by the destination. I will also frequently change destinations as the terrain becomes clearer and clearer. The way that things appear isn't as important as ensuring that they are simple, beautiful and elegant. If your Melancholic mind goes into a loop over that last statement, then, tough luck!

I need creative activity to be able to explore my depths, and to learn and develop my capacity to communicate my insights and thoughts. Without a creative expression my thoughts will often become unclear to me, and I will struggle to articulate them. Creative navigation usually becomes more important than the arrival because the oceans are deep and this enables me to see clearly. There must be integrated coherence to my projects or I will not be comfortable. The pieces must fit together, the intent must be pure and the journey staged and layered. The spirit of the journey must be manifest in its form, or it cannot be fulfilling and will result in a profound unease.

Contradictions get ironed out as I go. I smooth them out, optimise the congruences and examine the inconsistencies, frequently finding strengths there that I can make use of. Of course, to the more logical types they may seem contradictory, but I have looked into their texture and impulse and I'm sure of the way they converge. My vantage point is the flow, what happens along the way, where it is going and how it is getting there. Therefore, I will look and observe at length as I work things out, and I may adjust things that to you appear unrelated, but in which I have perceived a profound interconnection.

My friends know that there is nowhere to hide. This is not because I am nosy, but my insight penetrates deeply, and so once I know you, I really know you, and I will find ways to support you before you even realise that you need it, and I expect you to trust that this is what I do. I'm quiet but good fun, and I'll always make sure that there is space for you to amuse yourself, whilst I sit on the sidelines and enjoy the show, with the occasional witty comment. Don't force me to be at the centre; it won't work.

My deep motivations must be given space to be expressed in the project, and this must involve people, nurturing people and balance. I need routine, I need flexibility and I will ensure that there is routine and flexibility. Growing things slowly ensures that this is built into the very fabric of things.

I need to feel connected to the things that I do in my life, connected to the people but able to stand aside. After connection comes passion, and I will often reassess things in order to protect my flexibility.

The Phlegmatic-Sanguine According to the World

You have such elegant style, but you don't really care about it! You are sensitive, intuitive and considerate. Your company is relaxing and you see everything and you just know where we are without us saying anything. Working with you is a pleasure unless we decide to force things along, you won't provoke a fight but you just disappear. If we ask questions and wait for the answers, whilst working with you, we build upon deep insight in quite surprising ways, which I wouldn't call unorthodox but we build from the fabric of the reality of things. Working with you from the perspective of pinning you down doesn't really work and that can be frustrating when we are Melancholics or Cholerics, who need things to be aimed towards clearly defined goals.

Getting you to talk and then waiting for you to do it is difficult and takes the development of herculean patience. Yes, it is hard but it pays its dividends if we persevere.

You have a strong sense of the sacred, harmonious and proper and you don't like it when we fail to respect these values, and you are prepared to cut off relations due to someone violating the sacrosanct, and you won't have very much to say. You just become unreachable.

And you are remarkably mature and wise.

The Phlegmatic-Sanguine Impulses

You dwell patiently in the depths of the Abyss, diving and sinking within it, and it is as if you must gather the swirling wind, to bring things to the surface. You employ the Sanguine to fulfil your Phlegmatic needs, you may speak and interact to observe more deeply beneath the surface, interact with people to fulfil your need for stability and safety and find the nurturing spaces to quietly encourage interaction. You need harmony and harmony seeks you. The effort of bringing the new to the surface is an exhausting endeavour and you need space to renew and reinvigorate.

You need environments which allow you to sit on the sidelines whilst they nurture you as you nurture them. Your creative expression is more of a swimming within the depths to see the deep pattern and then you bring it to the surface and so your creative work has deep connections and insights, and as a result you are not interested at all in the superficial.

Your patience is legendary because in your core you are already contented even when discontentment overwhelms you. Things have no parts; they are a connected flow and so you tease their impulses out as they manifest in their layered emergence.

You need to sit still to gather the force to move. Then you need to be still to gather the wind to bring it from the depths of the Abyss.

Summary

This is a deeply introverted type who dwells in their depths and comes occasionally to the surface. Self contained and able to stand aside whilst remaining involved. They need deep involvement and empathy and have a profound emotional life and so can be wounded very deeply. This type requires a reliable sense of safety to be encouraged to come to the surface. They will not connect if they don't feel safe and their relationships require gentleness, patience and the protection of their boundaries. Creativity is necessary for their sanity and emotional balance. If you seek connection with them then give them space, safety and a creative playful place for them from which to establish relationships. Remember that they will establish a connection with you, not the other way around. You have to maintain a space for them to accomplish this.

The Phlegmatic-Choleric

The Phlegmatic-Choleric is a Phlegmatic who expresses strong Choleric traits, they are empathetic and loyal, with Choleric traits often employed to protect and facilitate the Phlegmatic. The strong consistent intuition of the Phlegmatic, combined with swift Choleric judgement resulting in what I can only call intuitive judgement, with bucket loads of empathy. The cold and wet of the Elemental Water combines with the hot and dry of the Elemental Fire to result in a non-complementary nature which works well when they are well, but will appear bipolar when they are not. They more even tempered than the Choleric-Phlegmatic and their anger is not as hot, but it tends to burn slowly and may last longer when they are well and shorter when they are not well. This type requires acres of space and is naturally very flexible, searching with a peculiar focus that enhances their explorational flexibility.

The phlegmatic's observing, reserved and questioning nature ensures that this is not a goal oriented type but that they possess focus. Rather than looking for optimum results this type looks for integrity, a sense of connectedness and wholeness in all that they do.

Water heated by fire results in steam and this is a type that can actually be quite sanguine but must be very comfortable and well to manifest this. Their reserve may suddenly vanish and they overflow with sanguine conversation and curiosity though you may never see them, speaking without thinking of the way it will be interpreted as sanguines do. This type doesn't ever really put their foot in it, even when quite sanguine. This type won't generally be sanguine in crowds unless with a group that they know really well and are exceedingly comfortable with, or alternatively they are incredibly happy. Since the Sanguine doesn't drive the impulse they can turn it off in a flash to return to their Phlegmatic reserve.

They are shockingly empathetic, reserved and competent and have the capacity to make swift cutting judgements when threatened. At this point they will be fierce and overpowering. If they are forced into a prolonged period of threat they will draw hard boundaries and they will protect them fiercely.

They need to really stand apart, on the sidelines, and they need clarity. The fire serves this purpose. They need to flow around obstacles and will avoid confrontation, with a natural restraint that is at its root a sign of wisdom.

This is a deeply nurturing type with natural boundaries and a capacity for fierceness. Then they disappear.

The World According to the Phlegmatic-Choleric

I observe first and listen later, and trust what people say much less than what they do. I need to be still and to observe from the margins and will emerge into the open when I am comfortable and will use my natural boundaries to create the space to observe and ensure that my boundaries are respected. When I've seen enough and decided to act I can do this decisively, smoothly and easily though I tend to be apprehensive, but I've noticed that others don't seem to notice. I feel my way through the world, and so my intuition leads my judgement, and I act based upon what I feel having paid long and close attention. Once situations have revealed consistent patterns, I will act and usually decisively, I flow, feel and strike my way rhythmically to the solution, with a sensitivity of feeling and wholeness which guides my determination.

My strength dwells in my depths and I need to allow it to gather and move according to currents which flow well below the surface. I move the situation by employing passive strategies decisively. I will use gentleness and entice people to act by loading the circumstances into well curated patterns that suit my *modus operandi*. I don't wear a velvet glove, it is as if I have velvet hands with steel fingers and so I will rarely go head to head with an antagonist, but I can if I must.

I make life easy for myself and those around me and don't take kindly to anyone making life difficult for me. They usually find themselves out of my sphere fairly quickly, when I am well and standing within my power.

The Phlegmatic-Choleric Traits in The Eyes of the World

Your movements are elegant, smooth, connected, gentle and strong, though you remain just beyond our reach unless you decide to let us in, and you need to look long and carefully before you decide. Conversations tend to be long, honest and deep and you really don't have time for small talk. It just doesn't work for you. Your insights seek the depths, but you are apprehensive of those seeking to penetrate those depths before you are ready. This is a trait of all Phlegmatics, but your sense of boundaries makes it quite noticeable. You need lots of time to reflect, regather and to swim alone in your own depths. Your boundaries tend to be soft but thick, you use moats rather than walls, and you might put some decorated thorny hedges around the circumference. People have to make their way across the moat whilst you observe them.

Your way with projects is by feeling your way through as you swim, twist and leap occasionally from the depths with some pearl unexpectedly found, at which point we need to listen. Your close friends will do a fair amount of listening as the water turns to sanguine steam and you explore your depths in the mirror of your friends. We did say friends, but they will tend to be fewer than five. In fact five is a lot. More like three.

The Phlegmatic-Choleric Impulses

You swim in the deep, searching, diving and relaxing in the depths of the abyss. The music of the depths sings through you and you disappear within it. Not so much exploring as being in the depths often with a playfulness that would surprise others. It really has to grip and possess you for you to swim up to the surface to bring it into the world. What you see is more for you than for them, and you aren't that interested in reaching many people but would love a sense of connectedness with like minds that you know, who you are able to know at a glance. And do the rest really need to understand? Well they might but is that really your responsibility? Here is where you are split between empathy and your desire to swim comfortably back into the depths, but the depths usually win.

Your hidden song gathers and grips you, with an almost sexual fire until you must sing it and then you sing it coolly to the end, leaving it for those who would like to listen and not really caring about the rest. If it lights the song of another that would be great, but then it is now their song, so let them sing it. You prefer to work alone.

You don't want your freedom, you already have it and it is within you and you know it.

Summary

This is a quiet self contained Phlegmatic, who has a deep sense of confidence and apprehension, both coiling in their depths. To swim out of the depths the passion for the thing has to overcome the apprehension so don't expect copious output, but deep, considered living and a need for connected meaningful lifework. They don't relate easily and are very picky about their friends and companions and they have to be able to plumb the depths. They keep themselves to themselves.

The Phlegmatic-Melancholic

I dwell in the depth of my waters, quietly for there the music is strong, sweeping and imagination causes the deep caverns to glitter with stars, jewels and treasures that I don't even care to share. I will not be teased out of the depths unless I wish to be, and when I do, if I choose to share the treasures with you, they, like the jewels of the cavernous depths, are brilliant and marvellously made. I am the waters at the centre of the earth, they know my name and I know theirs, with a shocking intimacy that does not need words but then comes my Melancholic nature and it must speak them quietly, logically and clearly, but you would be mistaken if you thought that they are logically arrived at. No, they are the gifts of insight, intuition and imagination. That is why I prefer the hidden underground worlds of the water's depths. I dwell in the depths of the abyss and though I am a Phlegmatic I am turned more to the depths than to seeking harmony with people. If you manage to be impressed by my insights before I've written them in a book, poetry or a painting, then you must really know how to dive and have been able to divine from the smallest appearances the greatness of the depths and the worlds that emerge.

It isn't that I cannot be contained but that I do not surface long enough for you to even get hold of me. My connection is in my depths and I rarely seek it in the world.

Leave me my space and I am not interested in yours. If you want to befriend me, then why would you even want to do that? If you are waiting for me to decide, I'm really not that interested. And if you want to make that connection then you'd better have a lot of time. I keep walls and moats and walls as boundaries and then I leave them alone as I dive and if you get past them then you are likely to find a labyrinth.

I am withdrawn, quiet, imaginative, thoughtful, reflective and self-contained. I don't do much in the world and you may think that there is not much to find, and that suits me fine. There are worlds beneath the bonnet and bonnets beneath the worlds. I'm not particularly interested in connecting with you and I'm really quite apprehensive of relationships.

It isn't that I need to dive, I'm a diver and that is what I am made to do. Yes, I have a sense of humour, I'm socially awkward and it suits me fine. Now if I find a creature who can swim in the depths and communicate succinctly, reading the hidden in what I have to say, that creature will win my heart. They are often possible in my opposite and that will baffle me and I will crave their mystery and then I may come up apprehensively from my dives. But I'm not particularly good at empathy, even though I am a Phlegmatic, but I do have some.

My deep capacity for intuitive and intellectual endeavours, means that I need great thorny questions to explore, creatively and with the intellectual tools of a scholar warrior. I explore and because I am not generally interested in speaking to others, the prose is written for me and tends to be thick and not focused upon accessibility. Within these two opposing forces magic happens and I catch the sparks at the centre of the world in the darkest depths and I nurture them until they become blazing illuminating fires. And I will always find a niche of interest with a surprising intuitive flexibility.

The Phlegmatic-Melancholic Traits in The Eyes of the World

You are hidden in the depths and we can't even reach you to figure you out, or even find the places to connect to you and if we wish to, it is a herculean task of patience and wisdom. There are very few who are capable of this. When we wish to play, you don't need to, and you're clearly not in need of us at all.

If we manage to get you to speak, then you do so sparingly, slowly and deliberately with the finesse of an artist and the strength of intellect of which there aren't many who can match up to it. Your secrets are hidden beneath the secrets which the world itself hides and you are inaccessible and if you finally invite us in, then we have to enter your world and you are rarely interested in ours.

You are well mannered and keep us at a distance so that you may dive back into your depths. There are truly very few that you take into your confidence and then you are shockingly loyal. But whoever breaks that trust has forever fallen beyond the pale.

To speak with you in conversation, give time, ask questions, turn it around and consider, this one will not suffer fools gladly or feign interest.

Expect diagrams and explanations, then if you connect, a glint in their eyes will finally flash and it all comes flooding out, but if we interrupt it we may never be able to make that connection again. If we manage to connect and weather this initial deluge, then somehow we find ourselves swept into your confidence.

In working relationships you work at your own pace and on your own things. The depth, thoroughness and insight is mindblowing but keeping you on track is difficult. And you don't tend to speak up about problems, you just change direction and break contact.

The Phlegmatic-Melancholic Impulses

Within the cavernous deeps of the abyss you will be found. Diving into possibilities and dwelling alone within unfathomable caves. At these depths your imagination illuminates the darkness and you scarcely need to resurface for sunlight . The treasures that lie below the surface are sufficient for you, and refusing to be earthbound, you explore them in a continuous internal conversation with yourself.

The hidden songs possess you, and you know them before you hear them and you must hear them to know them. You gaze intuitively upon their essence by means of your Phlegmatic aspect and logically unfold their complexity by your Melancholic aspect.

There are few who can follow you in this but you will be eternally isolated if you do not find them.

Summary

This is a type which requires the depths and must have rigorous intuitive and intellectual challenge if life is not to become uninteresting for them. They need lots of space and they thrive on picking apart thorny challenges that suit their preference for working on their own. They are driven by curiosity. You have to win their trust and their respect for your intellect and intuition before they invite you in.

Putting It All Together

We have explored the Phlegmatic and its three patterns of emergence. Their easygoing, quiet, observant and diplomatic dislike of conflict, is well known for those who take the time to notice them. Their loyalty, quiet promotion of harmony and capacity for listening without interrupting, often make them the water which allows the flexibility and communication that enable our families and societies to hold together. Yes! This is how they are wired and I hope that you have learned a lot about these highly intriguing figures in the pantheon of Elemental Types. If you have learned to improve your relationships with this fascinating type, and if they in turn have learned more about the value that they bring to the human story, then I am pleased to have provided you with an invaluable service.

Be patient with them, for they have almost certainly been patient with you.

The point of these books is that you develop an intuitive grasp of how to deal with the types, and in this case particularly, the Phlegmatic. Phlegmatics, I hope that you have achieved a more profound appreciation of the pattern of dynamics that animates you. I pray that this will help you to be a better Phlegmatic, or has taught you to better deal with Phlegmatics, as they inevitably slip through your fingers.

This is the last book on the biotypes in the Know Yourself series. The journey began in 2009 and has taken me 15 years to complete. Does that give you an important clue to working out what my own type is? You have the Bradford Literature Festival of 2024 to thank for this. They asked me to complete the series in time for my participation in the festival. Please continue to dip into the series and explore the types, they were written to support us in learning to better deal with each other. It is often the drama and trauma that we inflict upon each other in relationships that is responsible for much of our mental and physical illness (they are not separate). People are difficult to deal with and learning to be better at dealing with ourselves and others is the key that opens the way to begin to readjust the settings of the totality of human relationships.

My dear Phlegmatic, you will require a particular form of courage in order for you to fulfil your most important and vital social role, but you must engage with this holding space for compassion towards yourself. You are already incredibly empathetic in your relations with others. Your dragons and demons lie deep within the depths of your waters, and this is all very well, but you must dive and work to unearth those invaluable treasures and then bring them to the surface. It is hard work and that is the texture of life itself.

Failure is the necessary companion on the journey to success. Success, when it arrives, has been built in the depths and what people see and value is often so little of the vast travails which lie concealed in the depths. Gentle, empathetic persistence brings forth a humane, benevolent and genial assemblage. In our age, idealism has been responsible for the most self-righteous tyrannies, utterly blinded by idealism. You, the Phlegmatic, have many gifts to bring to the social relations which make up the transactional material of society.

Here is a summary of the important lessons of this book:

1. Work with yourself and not against yourself: you are yourself and not another. You can only build with and upon what you have. Stop wishing that you were someone else, because you aren't, and begin working with what you have been given. You've already got it so why try to work with what you don't have and cry when you fail? Get to know yourself very, very well and that necessitates exposing yourself to varying situations which will expose you to your own hidden aspects.

2. Understand your default reactions, what triggers them and how they unfold. Don't worry about the why, dwell in the how, for often when you do that consistently the why declares itself by itself. Learn when your default reactions are appropriate and when they are not and learn to work with yourself to bring appropriateness. This is the fabric of wisdom.

3. Other types have their strengths, and you have yours. Learn from others. Otto von Bismarck, the first Chancellor of the German Empire reportedly said, "Fools say that they learn by experience. I prefer to profit from the experience of others."

Learn from them, copy them and benefit from their natural genius. In this way you will add new strategies and tactics to your toolbox.

4. Observe, reflect, change and repeat the process. Don't expect to get it right the first time, rather, focus upon coming closer to the mark with each cycle. This will introduce a fundamental flexibility into your journey and will allow you to act and not depend upon mustering tremendous courage and will every time. This allows you to live and change in smaller, more manageable cycles. Be gentle with yourself, because life is already hard enough without you having to make it even more difficult.

Existence is woven marvellously and observation will leave you dazzled at the remarkable ingenuity, beauty and interconnection of the handiwork. The Four Elements is a wisdom for working with the patterns of the creation, to learn to unfold its potentialities, possibilities and outcomes. Yes, we will and should get it wrong, on the journey to getting it right. Celebrate both your victories and your failures. For your failures celebrate that this is not a place that you will be stopping at again, and of your victories ask for more.

People are what they are. You are what you are. You can't make bananas into mangoes, apples into grapes or snakes into monkeys. Focus upon changing what you can; and the person over whom you have the most capacity to change is yourself. So change yourself and you will see that this is usually enough for others to be forced to change (even if it is only to adjust to you). Learn from the errors and faults of others and do the hard everyday work on yourself.

So let's make life interesting with the variety, arrayed across the world for us to explore and the differences between people and peoples for us to embrace. Accept them and learn from the vast differences. See yourself in their reflection and give them space to see themselves in the mirror that you provide. You will see different perspectives, learn the strength of variety and see that the chaos is patterned and brings forth unexpected openings. These attitudes force you to really interrogate yourself, your assumptions, presumptions and perspectives and in this you will discover that differences are a mercy. Often, the place you'll see this most clearly is in the culinary world.

But remember that always changing yourself, changes what is around you, and this radiates out into the universe.

"Cultivate virtue in yourself, and virtue will be real.

Cultivate it in the family, and virtue will abound.

Cultivate it in the village, and virtue will grow.

Cultivate it in the nation, and virtue will be abundant.

Cultivate it in the universe, and virtue will be everywhere."

-- Tao te Ching, Lao Tze

Phlegmatics are a gift!

www.ingramcontent.com/pod-product-compliance
Lightning Source LLC
Chambersburg PA
CBHW072009040426
42447CB00009B/1550